WORLD HISTORY ATLAS

A collection of maps illustrating geographically the most significant periods and events in the history of civilization.

CONTENTS

Published by **HAMMOND** INCORPORATED **MAPLEWOOD, NEW JERSEY**

Printed in U.S.A.

PREHISTORIC MAN

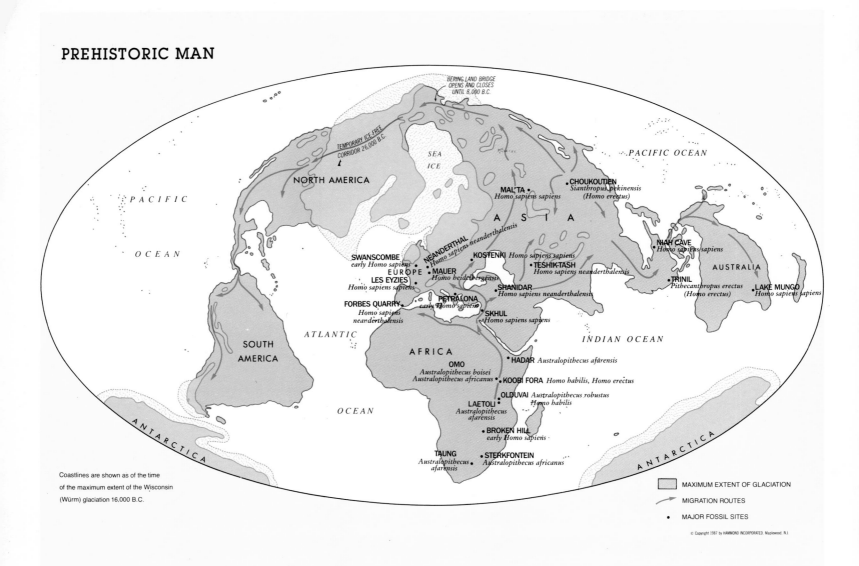

Coastlines are shown as of the time
of the maximum extent of the Wisconsin
(Würm) glaciation 16,000 B.C.

MAXIMUM EXTENT OF GLACIATION

MIGRATION ROUTES

MAJOR FOSSIL SITES

© Copyright 1987 by HAMMOND INCORPORATED, Maplewood, N.J.

THE SPREAD OF FARMING AND EARLY DOMESTICATION OF CROPS AND ANIMALS

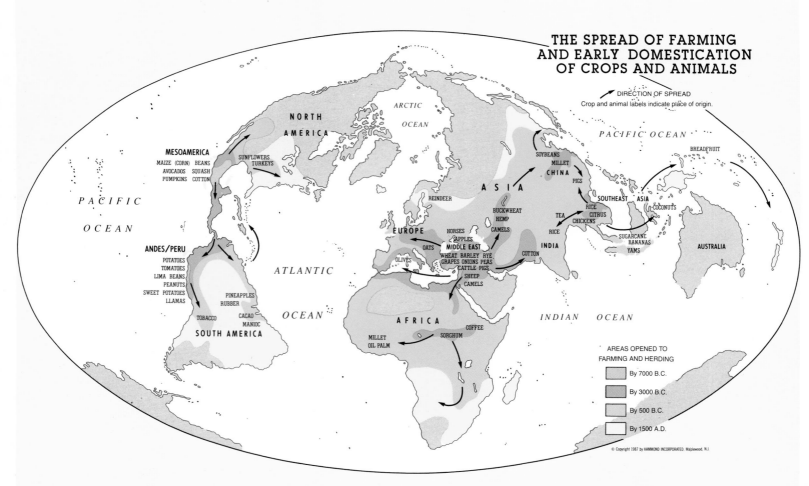

DIRECTION OF SPREAD
Crop and animal labels indicate place of origin.

AREAS OPENED TO
FARMING AND HERDING

By 7000 B.C.

By 3000 B.C.

By 500 B.C.

By 1500 A.D.

© Copyright 1987 by HAMMOND INCORPORATED, Maplewood, N.J.

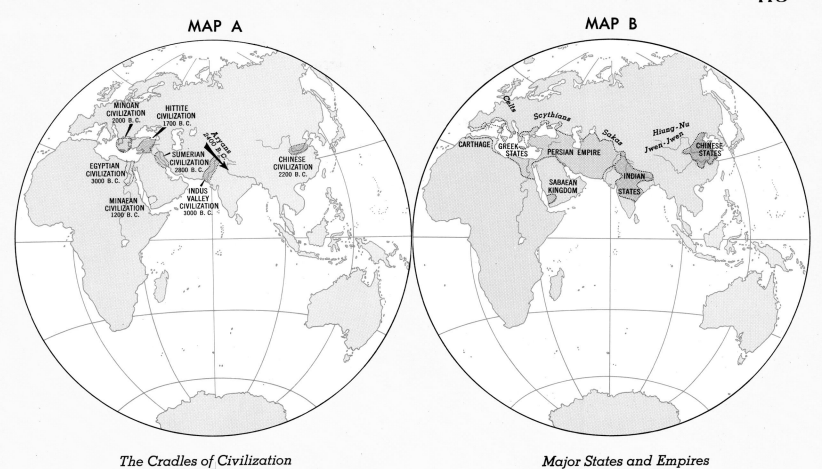

MAP A

The Cradles of Civilization
3000-1000 B.C.

MAP B

Major States and Empires
in 500 B.C.

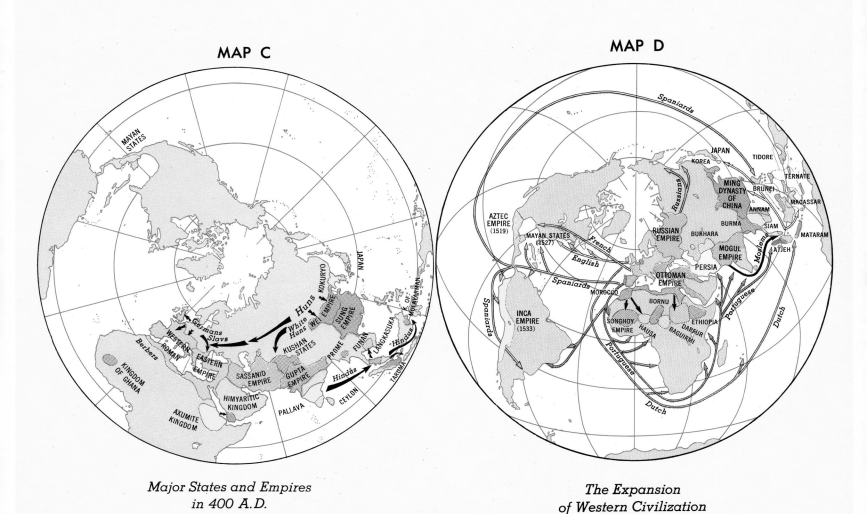

MAP C

Major States and Empires
in 400 A.D.

MAP D

The Expansion
of Western Civilization
1600 A.D.

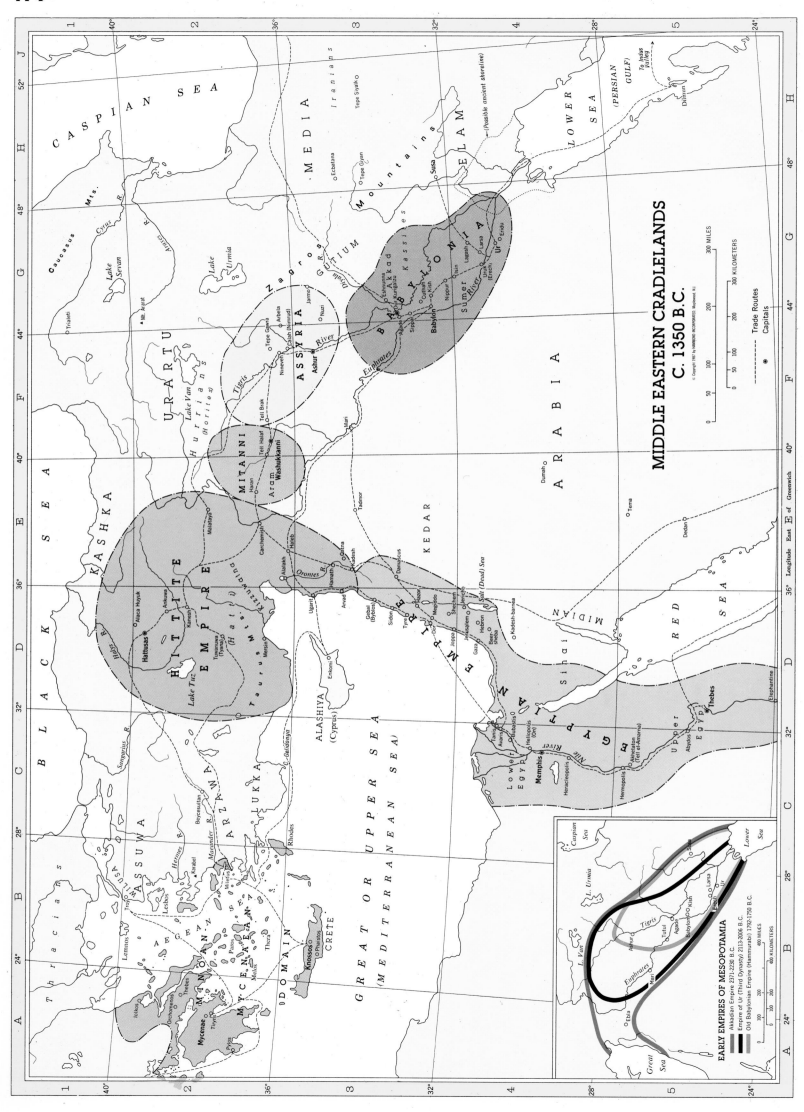

MIDDLE EASTERN CRADLELANDS
C. 1350 B.C.

© Copyright 1987 by HAMMOND INCORPORATED, Maplewood, N.J.

Trade Routes
Capitals

EARLY EMPIRES OF MESOPOTAMIA

Akkadian Empire 2371-2230 B.C.
Empire of Ur (Third Dynasty) 2113-2006 B.C.
Old Babylonian Empire (Hammurabi) 1792-1750 B.C.

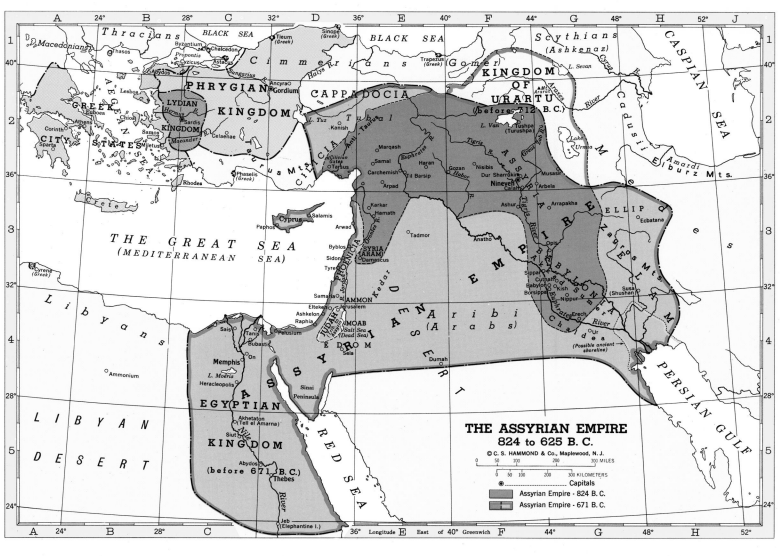

THE ASSYRIAN EMPIRE
824 to 625 B. C.

© C. S. HAMMOND & Co., Maplewood, N. J.

0 50 100 200 300 MILES
0 50 100 200 300 KILOMETERS

Capitals
Assyrian Empire - 824 B.C.
Assyrian Empire - 671 B.C.

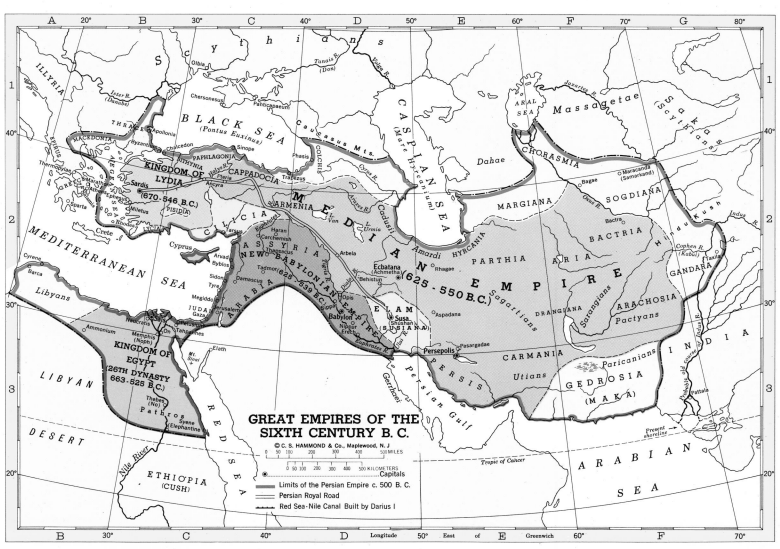

GREAT EMPIRES OF THE SIXTH CENTURY B. C.

© C. S. HAMMOND & Co., Maplewood, N. J.

0 50 100 200 300 400 500 MILES
0 50 100 200 300 400 500 KILOMETERS

Capitals
Limits of the Persian Empire c. 500 B. C.
Persian Royal Road
Red Sea-Nile Canal Built by Darius I

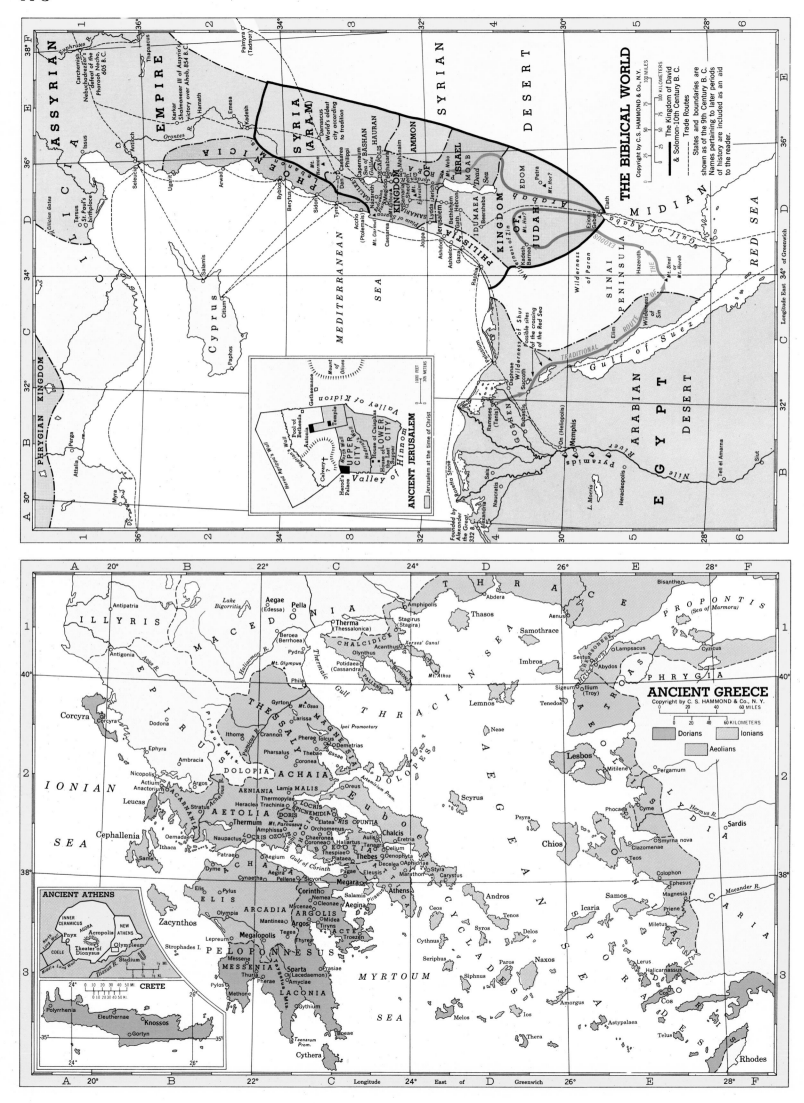

THE BIBLICAL WORLD

Copyright by C. S. Hammond & Co., N.Y.

— The Kingdom of David & Solomon-10th Century B.C.
········· Trade Routes

States and boundaries are shown as of the 9th Century B.C. Names pertaining to later periods of history are included as an aid to the reader.

ANCIENT JERUSALEM
Jerusalem at the time of Christ

ANCIENT GREECE

Copyright by C. S. Hammond & Co., N.Y.

Dorians   Ionians
Aeolians

ANCIENT ATHENS

CRETE

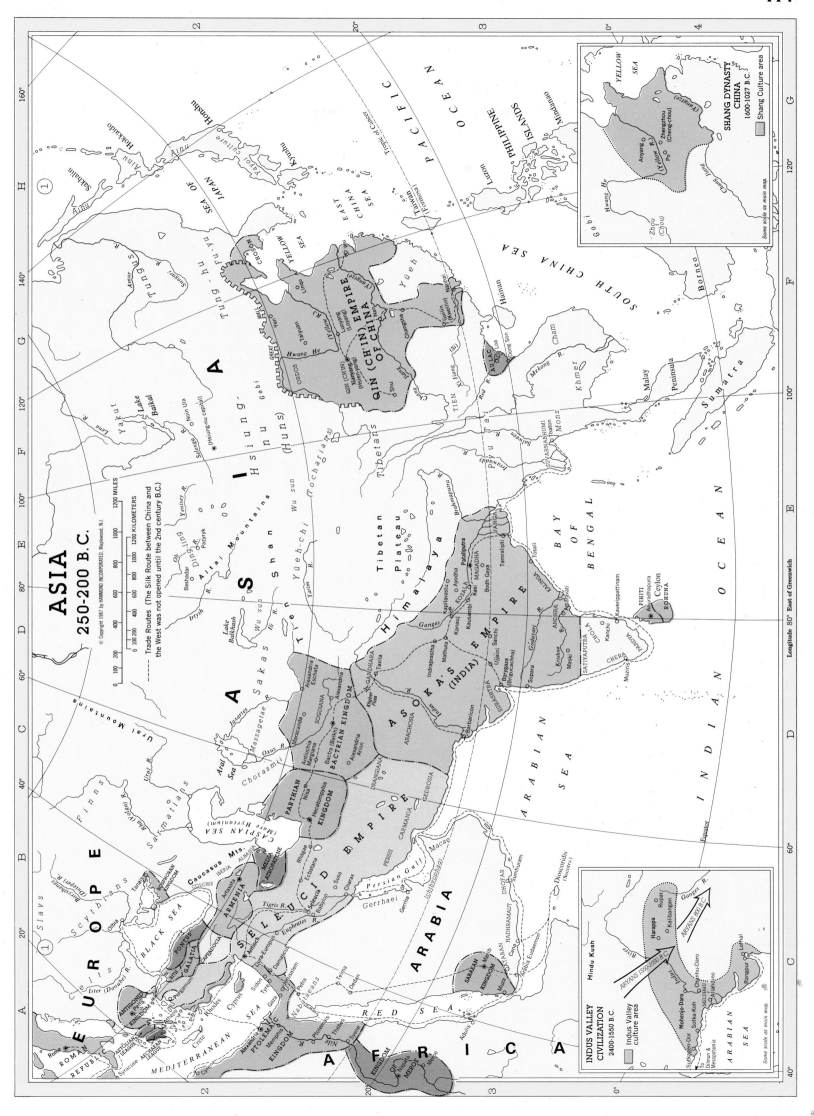

ASIA
250-200 B.C.

© Copyright 1987 by Hammond Incorporated, Maplewood, N.J.

—— Trade Routes (The Silk Route between China and
------ the West was not opened until the 2nd century B.C.)

0 100 200 400 600 800 1000 1200 MILES
0 100 200 400 600 800 1000 1200 KILOMETERS

SHANG DYNASTY CHINA
1600-1027 B.C.

YELLOW SEA

Anyang Zhengzhou (Cheng-chou)
Zhou (Chou) Po Chang Jiang

Hwang He (Yellow R.) Chang Jiang (Yangtze)

Gobi

☐ Shang Culture area

Same scale as main map.

INDUS VALLEY CIVILIZATION
2400-1550 B.C.

Hindu Kush

Harappa Rupar
Kalibangan
Indus River Ganges R.

ARYANS 1550-1050 B.C.

Mohenjo-Daro Chanhu-Daro
Sutkagen-Dor Sotka-Koh MELUHHA Alahdino
To Dilmun & Mesopotamia Lothal
Rangpur ARABIAN SEA

☐ Indus Valley culture area

Same scale as main map.

Longitude 80° East of Greenwich

EUROPE

ASIA

AFRICA

ARABIA

ROMAN REPUBLIC
Rome Syracuse

AETOLIAN LEAGUE
ACHAEAN LEAGUE

MEDITERRANEAN SEA

PTOLEMAIC KINGDOM
Alexandria Memphis

MEROE KINGDOM
Napata Meroe

RED SEA

Nile R.

SABAEAN KINGDOM
Marib Qataban

HADHRAMAUT DHOFAR

ARABIA Eudaemon
Cana Sumhuram

Dioscoridis (Socotra)

INDIAN OCEAN

ARABIAN SEA

SELEUCID EMPIRE

PARTHIAN KINGDOM
Nisa Hecatompylos

CASPIAN SEA (Mare Hyrcanium)

PONTUS GALATIA CAPPADOCIA
BITHYNIA PERGAMON KINGDOM
Pergamon Antioch Dura-Europus Damascus
Tyre Sidon Jerusalem Gaza Petra
Tarsus Antioch
Seleucia Babylon Susa Ecbatana
Ctesiphon Charax
PERSIS Persian Gulf Gerrha Gerrhaei
CARMANIA GEDROSIA

ARMENIA MEDIA ATROPATENE
Artaxata Rhagae

BLACK SEA
COLCHIS IBERIA ALBANIA
Caucasus Mts.
BOSPORAN KINGDOM
Tanais Olbia

Tigris R. Euphrates

BACTRIAN KINGDOM
Bactra (Balkh) Antiochia Margiana
Alexandria Arion
Maracanda SOGDIANA
Alexandria Eschata
Khyber Pass
GANDHARA Taxila
Alexandria ARACHOSIA
DRANGIANA Khyber Pass

ASOKA'S EMPIRE (INDIA)
Indraprastha Mathura Kanauj Kausambi Ayodhya
KOSALA Kasi MAGADHA Pataliputra
Kapilavastu Sanchi Ujjain
Indus R. Ganges Bodh Gaya
Barbaricon Sopara Barygaza (Bhrigucachha)
ANDHRA Godavari Krishna Amaravati
KALINGA Tosali Tamralipti
Maski CHERA CHOLA Kanchi
SATIYAPUTRA PANDYA Kaveripattinam Muziris

BAY OF BENGAL

Ceylon
PIHITI Anuradhapura
ROHUNA

Scythians Sarmatians Massagetae
Aral Sea Jaxartes Oxus Chorasmi
Sakas Wu sun Tien Shan
Lake Balkhash Ili R. Tarim R.
Wu sun Yüeh-chi (Tocharians)

Slavs Finns Ural Mountains
Ural R. Volga R. (Rha) Dnieper R. (Borysthenes)
Obi R. Irtysh Yenisei Lena R.
Yakut Lake Baikal
Selenge Noin Ula (Hsiung-nu capital)

A S I A

Hsiung-nu (Huns) Gobi ORDOS

Tibetans Tibetan Plateau
Himalaya Brahmaputra
Irrawaddy Salween Mekong R.
Khmer Cham Dong Son
SUVARNABHUMI Thaton Mons
Malay Peninsula Sumatra Borneo

QIN (CHIN) EMPIRE OF CHINA
Qin (Chin) Xianyang (Hsienyang)
Hwang He Taiyuan Yen CHOSON
Luoyang (Loyang) Linzi
Yangtze R. Yen Yueh
Shu Chengdu Changsha Nanhai
Guilin (Kweilin) Xi Jiang (Si)
TIEN AU LAC Red R. Loa

YELLOW SEA EAST CHINA SEA
SOUTH CHINA SEA
PACIFIC OCEAN

JAPAN SEA OF JAPAN
Sakhalin Hokkaido Honshu Kyushu Ainu
Ainu culture Yayoi culture
Tung-hu (Tung-hu) Amur R. Sungari Ussuri

PHILIPPINE ISLANDS
Luzon Mindoro Mindanao
Taiwan (Formosa) Hainan

Tropic of Cancer Equator

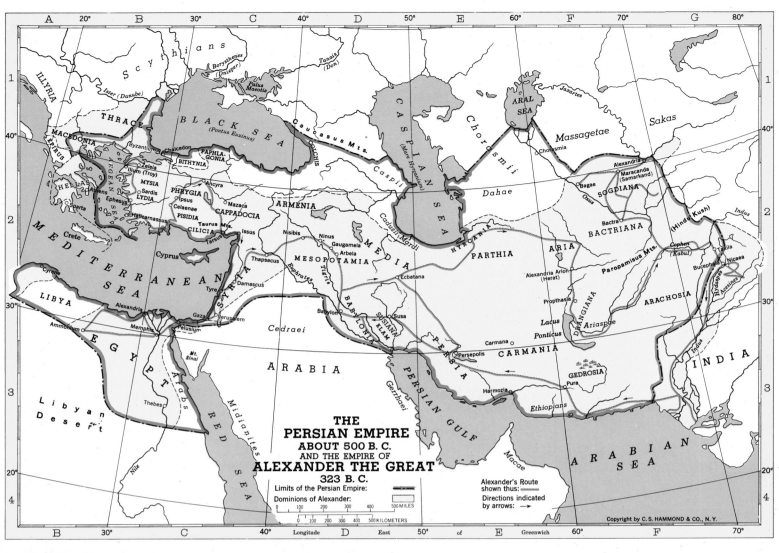

THE PERSIAN EMPIRE
ABOUT 500 B. C.
AND THE EMPIRE OF
ALEXANDER THE GREAT
323 B. C.

Limits of the Persian Empire:
Dominions of Alexander:

Alexander's Route
shown thus:
Directions indicated
by arrows: →

0 100 200 300 400 500 MILES
0 100 200 300 400 500 KILOMETERS

Longitude   East   of   Greenwich

Copyright by C. S. HAMMOND & CO., N. Y.

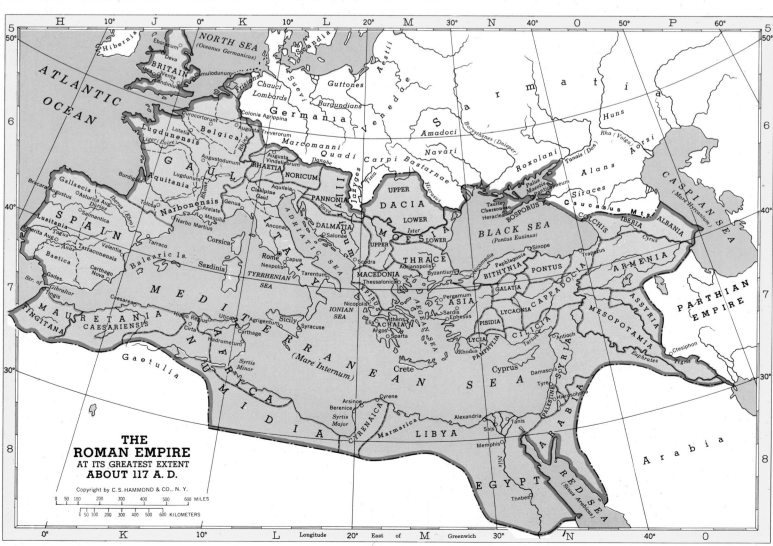

THE ROMAN EMPIRE
AT ITS GREATEST EXTENT
ABOUT 117 A. D.

Copyright by C. S. HAMMOND & CO., N. Y.

0 50 100 200 300 400 500 600 MILES
0 50 100 200 300 400 500 600 KILOMETERS

Longitude   East   of   Greenwich

ANCIENT ITALY
ITALIA, LIGURIA, VENETIA, GALLIA-CISALPINA, HISTRIA, SICILIA & CORSICA
Before the time of Augustus

Copyright by C.S. HAMMOND & CO., N.Y.

Roman Colonies, thus: ------- Ostia
Greek Colonies, thus: --- SYRACUSAE (G)
Carthaginian Colonies, thus: _____ Eryx (C)
Dotted lines show the Modern shore line

THE FORUM CAPITOLIUM and PALATIUM
1. Templum Saturni
2. Templum Concordiae
3. Scalae Gemoniae
4. Carcer (Tullianum)
5. Senaculum
6. Graecostasis
7. Rostra
8. Templum Jani

IMPERIAL FORA
1. Scalae Gemoniae
2. Templum Vespasiani
3. Porticus Deorum Consentium
4. Equus Caesaris
5. T. Castoris et Pollucis
6. Templum Divi Julii
7. Arcus Augusti
8. Arcus Titi
9. Templum Antonini et Faustinae

ROME
Under the Emperors
1. Templum Jovis Capitolini
2. Arx
3. Forum Romanum
4. Templum Aesculapii
5. Forum Trajani
6. Forum Augusti
7. Porta Carmentalis
8. Arcus Septimii Severi
9. Arcus Constantini
10. Arcus Titi
11. Arcus Claudii
12. Arcus Tiberii
13. Arcus Gallieni
14. Arcus Marci Aurelii
15. Arcus Diocletiani
16. Porta Flumentara
17. Templum Mercurii
18. Theatrum Marcelli

REGIONES AUGUSTI
I. Porta Capena
II. Caelimontium
III. Isis et Serapis
IV. Templum Pacis
V. Esquiliae
VI. Alta Semita
VII. Via Lata
VIII. Forum Romanum
IX. Circus Flaminius
X. Palatium
XI. Circus Maximus
XII. Piscina Publica
XIII. Aventinus
XIV. Trans Tiberim

ROME
In the time of the Republic

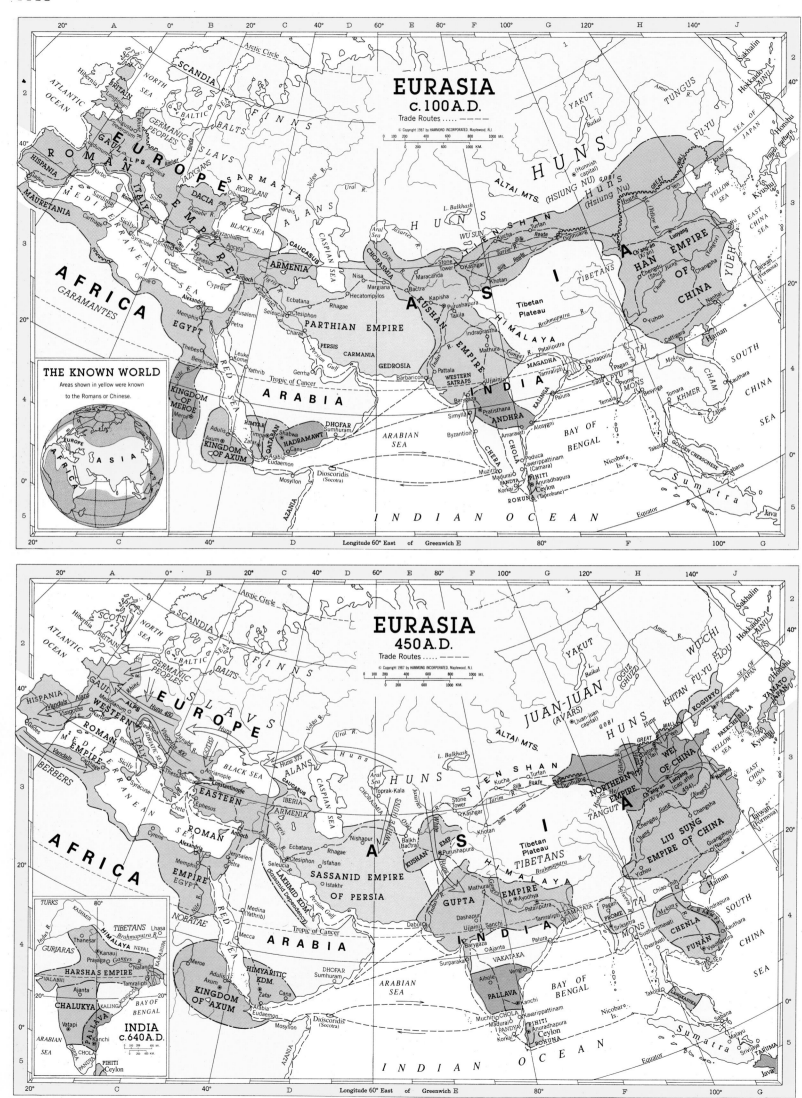

EURASIA
c.100 A.D.
Trade Routes .....

THE KNOWN WORLD
Areas shown in yellow were known
to the Romans or Chinese.

EURASIA
450 A.D.
Trade Routes .....

INDIA
c.640 A.D.

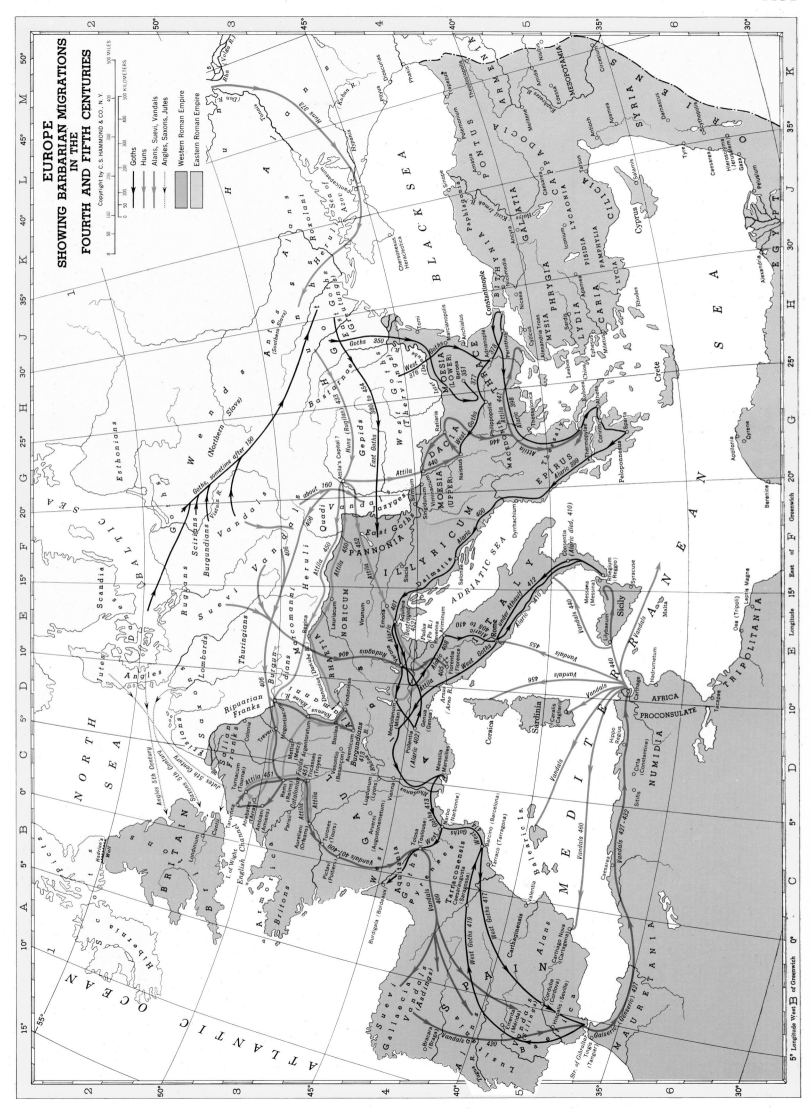

EUROPE
SHOWING BARBARIAN MIGRATIONS
IN THE
FOURTH AND FIFTH CENTURIES

Copyright by C. S. HAMMOND & CO., N.Y.

Goths
Huns
Alans, Suevi, Vandals
Angles, Saxons, Jutes
Western Roman Empire
Eastern Roman Empire

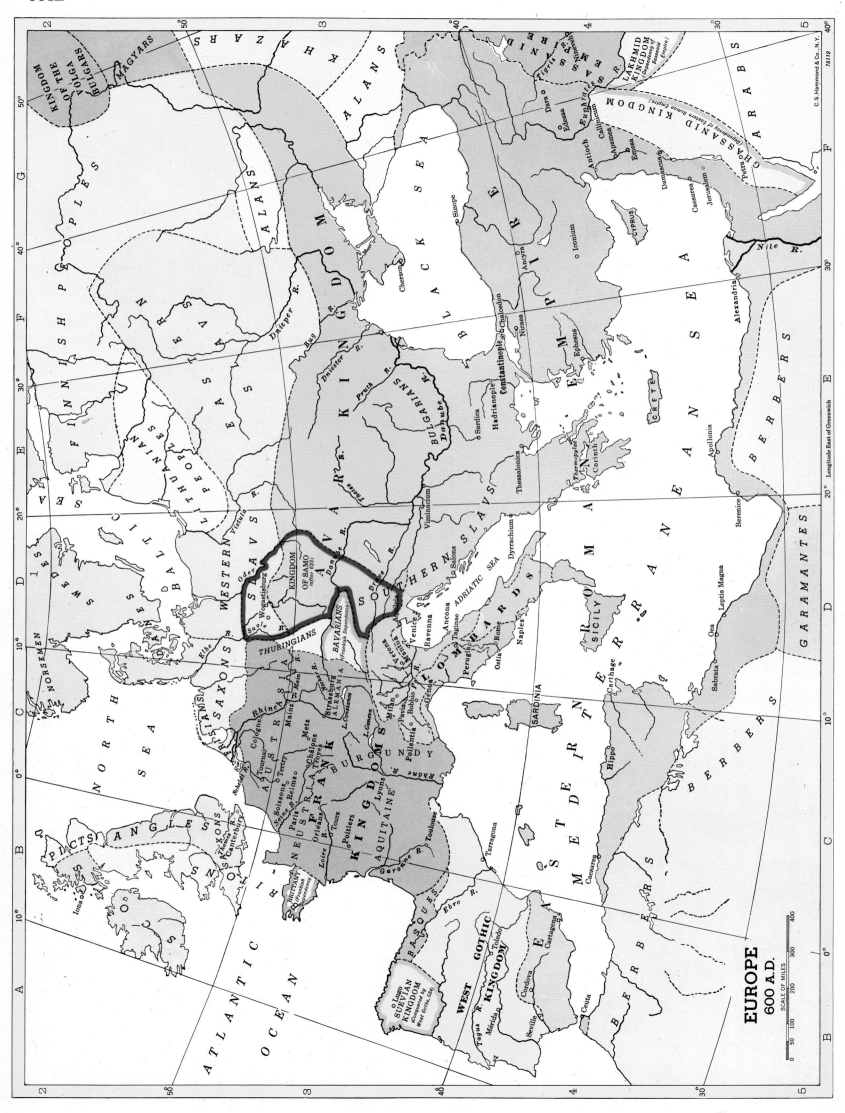

EUROPE
600 A.D.

SCALE OF MILES

0 50 100 200 300 400

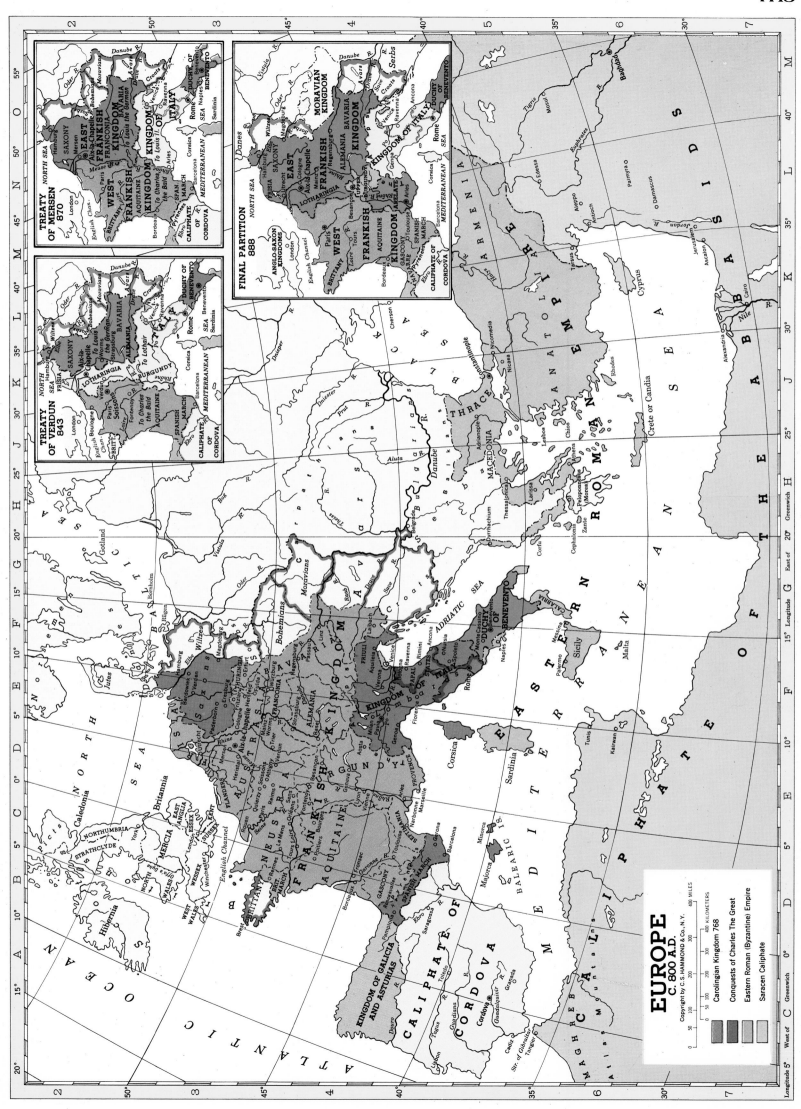

TREATY OF MERSEN 870

TREATY OF VERDUN 843

FINAL PARTITION 888

EUROPE
C. 800 A.D.

Copyright by C.S. HAMMOND & Co., N.Y.

Carolingian Kingdom 768
Conquests of Charles The Great
Eastern Roman (Byzantine) Empire
Saracen Caliphate

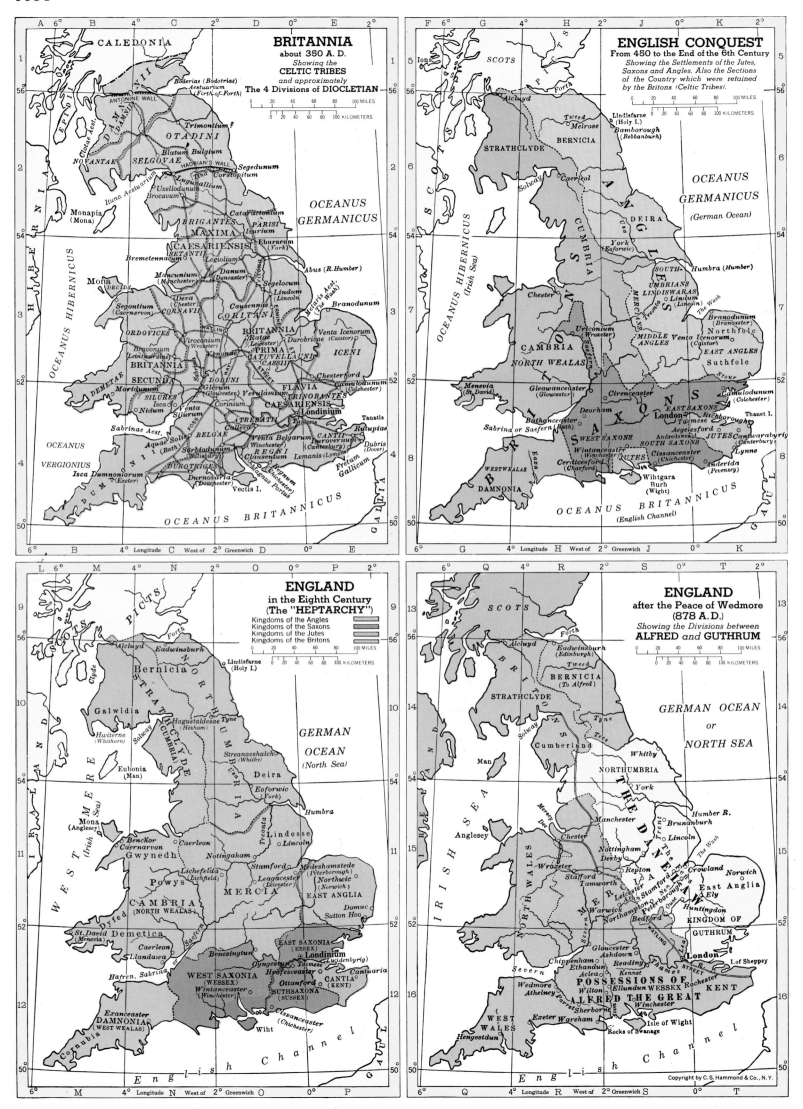

BRITANNIA
about 350 A. D.
Showing the
CELTIC TRIBES
and approximately
The 4 Divisions of DIOCLETIAN

ENGLISH CONQUEST
From 450 to the End of the 6th Century
*Showing the Settlements of the Jutes,
Saxons and Angles. Also the Sections
of the Country which were retained
by the Britons (Celtic Tribes).*

ENGLAND
in the Eighth Century
(The "HEPTARCHY")
Kingdoms of the Angles
Kingdoms of the Saxons
Kingdoms of the Jutes
Kingdoms of the Britons

ENGLAND
after the Peace of Wedmore
(878 A.D.)
Showing the Divisions between
ALFRED and GUTHRUM

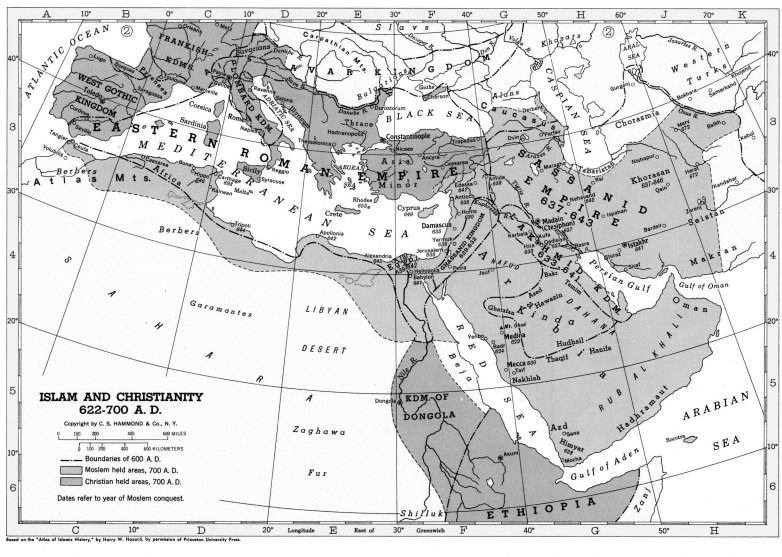

ISLAM AND CHRISTIANITY
622-700 A. D.

Copyright by C. S. HAMMOND & Co., N. Y.

0 100 200   400   600 MILES
0 100 200 400   600 KILOMETERS

—— Boundaries of 600 A. D.

Moslem held areas, 700 A. D.

Christian held areas, 700 A. D.

Dates refer to year of Moslem conquest.

Based on the "Atlas of Islamic History," by Harry W. Hazard, by permission of Princeton University Press.

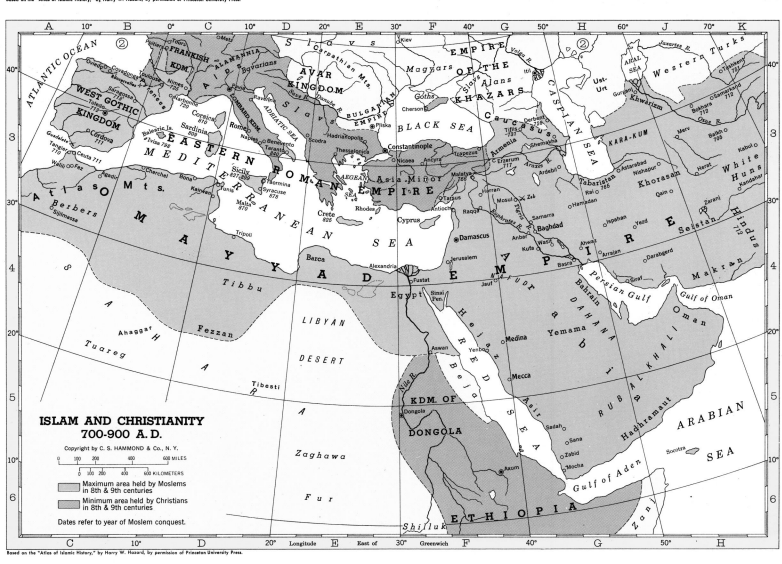

ISLAM AND CHRISTIANITY
700-900 A. D.

Copyright by C. S. HAMMOND & Co., N. Y.

0 100 200   400   600 MILES
0 100 200 400   600 KILOMETERS

Maximum area held by Moslems
in 8th & 9th centuries

Minimum area held by Christians
in 8th & 9th centuries

Dates refer to year of Moslem conquest.

Based on the "Atlas of Islamic History," by Harry W. Hazard, by permission of Princeton University Press.

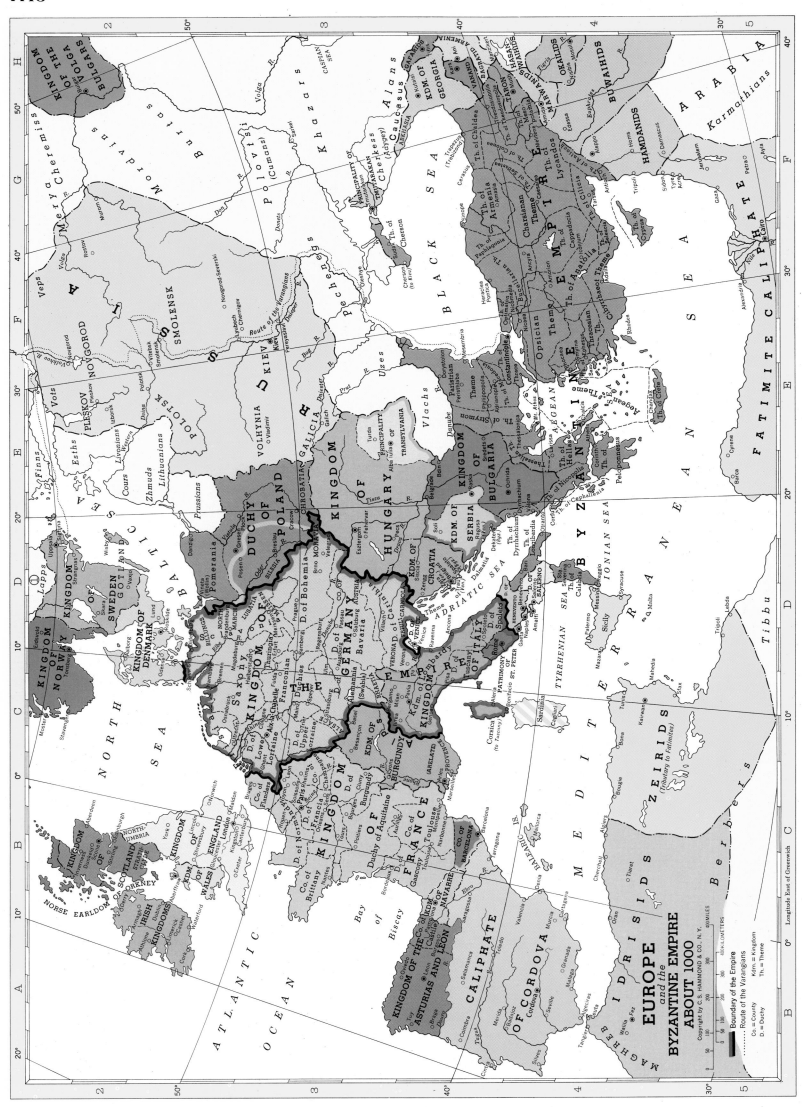

EUROPE
and the
BYZANTINE EMPIRE
ABOUT 1000

Copyright by C. S. HAMMOND & CO., N.Y.

Boundary of the Empire
Route of the Varangians

Co. = County   Kdm. = Kingdom
D. = Duchy   Th. = Theme

0 50 100 150 200 300 400 MILES
0 100 200 300 400 KILOMETERS

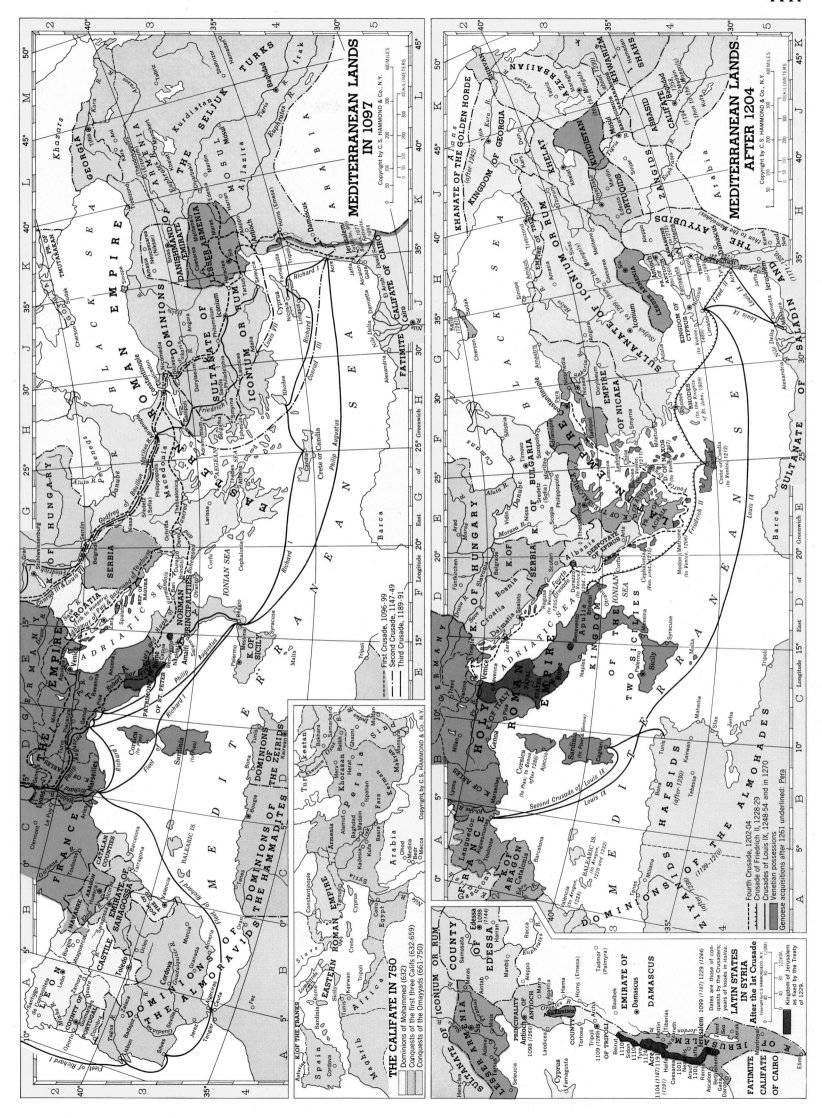

MEDITERRANEAN LANDS IN 1097

Copyright by C.S. HAMMOND & Co., N.Y.

First Crusade, 1096-99
Second Crusade, 1147-49
Third Crusade, 1189-91

THE CALIFATE IN 750

Copyright by C.S. HAMMOND & Co., N.Y.

Dominions of Mohammed (632)
Conquests of the first three Califs (632-659)
Conquests of the Omayyads (661-750)

MEDITERRANEAN LANDS AFTER 1204

Copyright by C.S. HAMMOND & Co., N.Y.

Fourth Crusade, 1202-04
Crusade of Friedrich II, 1228-29
Crusades of Louis IX, 1248-54 and in 1270
Venetian possessions after 1261 underlined: Pera
Genoese acquisitions after 1261 underlined

LATIN STATES IN SYRIA After the 1st Crusade

Copyright by C.S. HAMMOND & Co., N.Y.

Dates are those of conquests by the Crusaders; years of losses in italics.

Kingdom of Jerusalem as fixed by the Treaty of 1229.

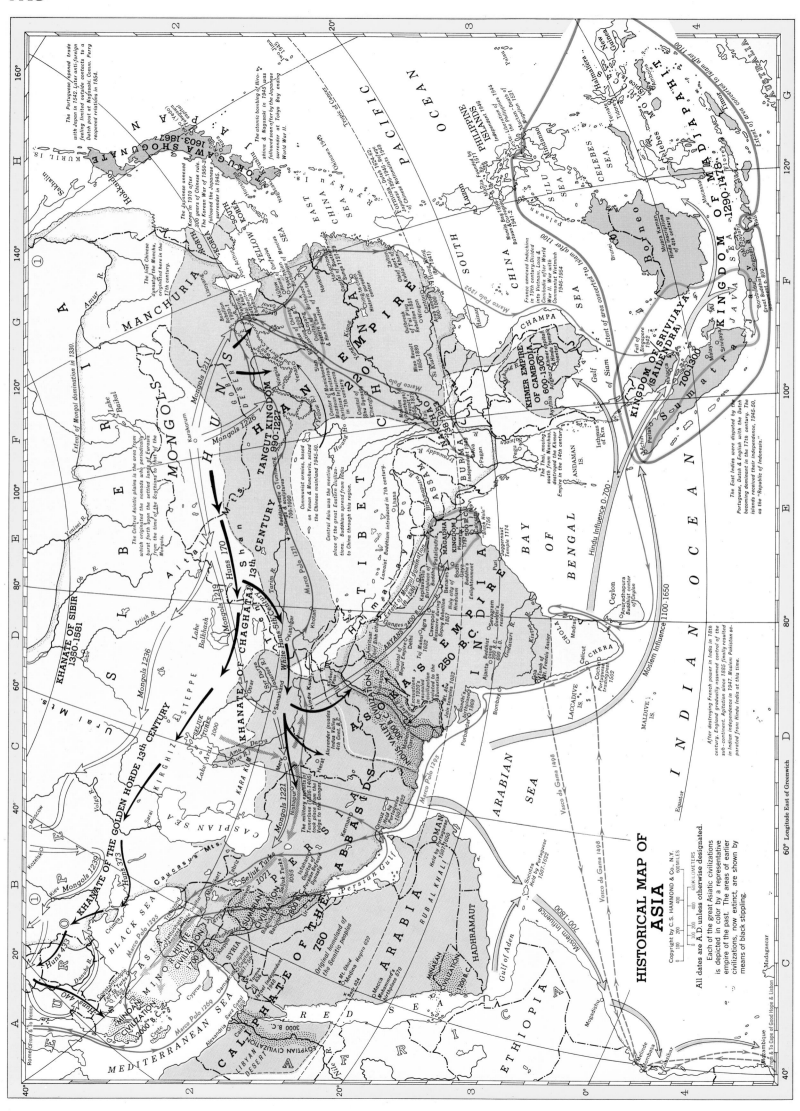

HISTORICAL MAP OF ASIA

Copyright by C.S. HAMMOND & Co., N.Y.

All dates are A.D. unless otherwise designated.

Each of the great Asiatic civilizations is depicted in color by a representative empire of the past. The areas of earlier civilizations, now extinct, are shown by means of black stippling.

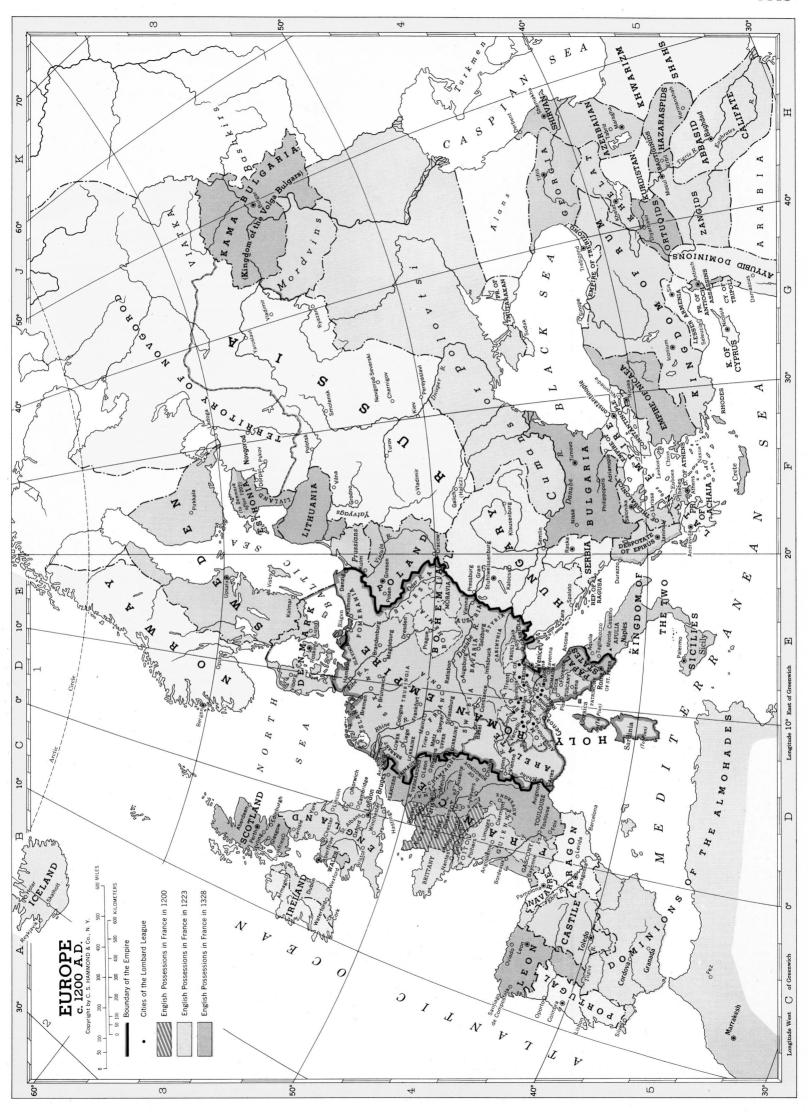

EUROPE
c. 1200 A.D.

Copyright by C. S. HAMMOND & Co., N.Y.

Boundary of the Empire

Cities of the Lombard League

English Possessions in France in 1200

English Possessions in France in 1223

English Possessions in France in 1328

MILES
0 100 200 300 400 500 600

0 100 200 300 400 500 600 KILOMETERS

Longitude 10° East of Greenwich

Longitude West 0° of Greenwich

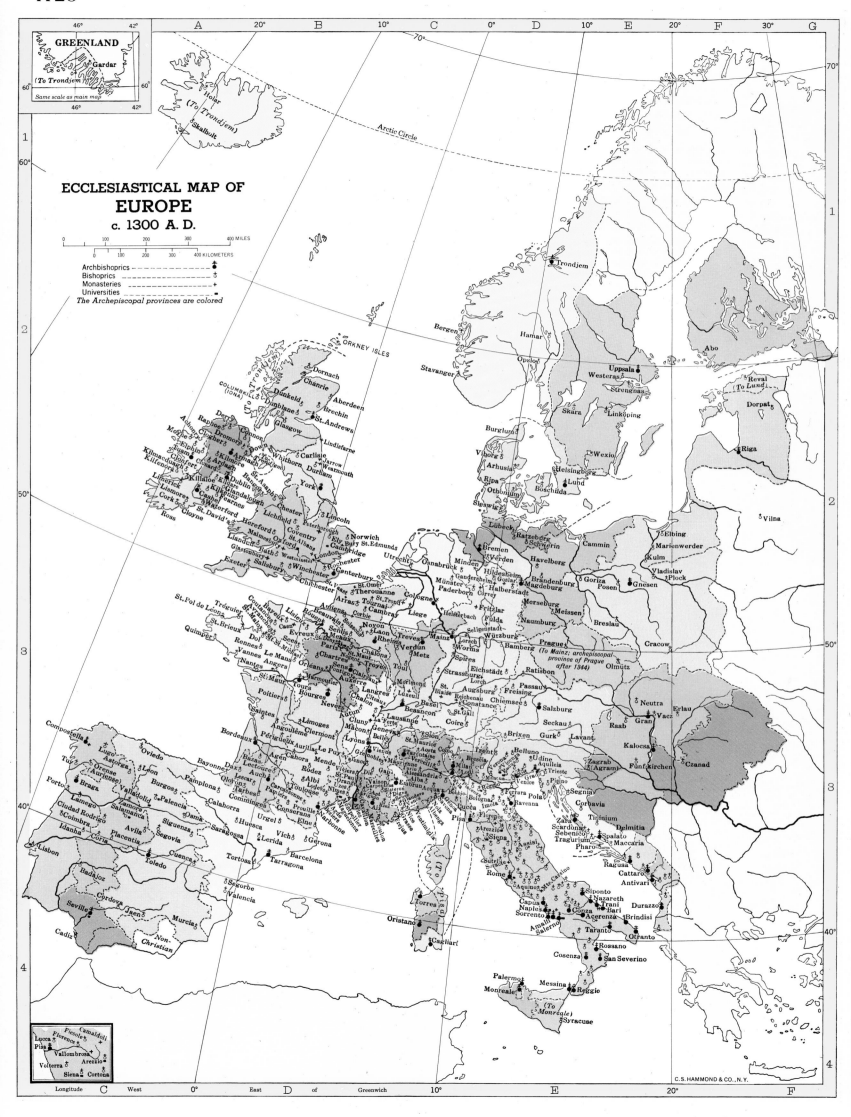

GREENLAND

Gardar

(To Trondjem)

Same scale as main map

ECCLESIASTICAL MAP OF
EUROPE
c. 1300 A.D.

Archbishoprics
Bishoprics
Monasteries
Universities
The Archepiscopal provinces are colored

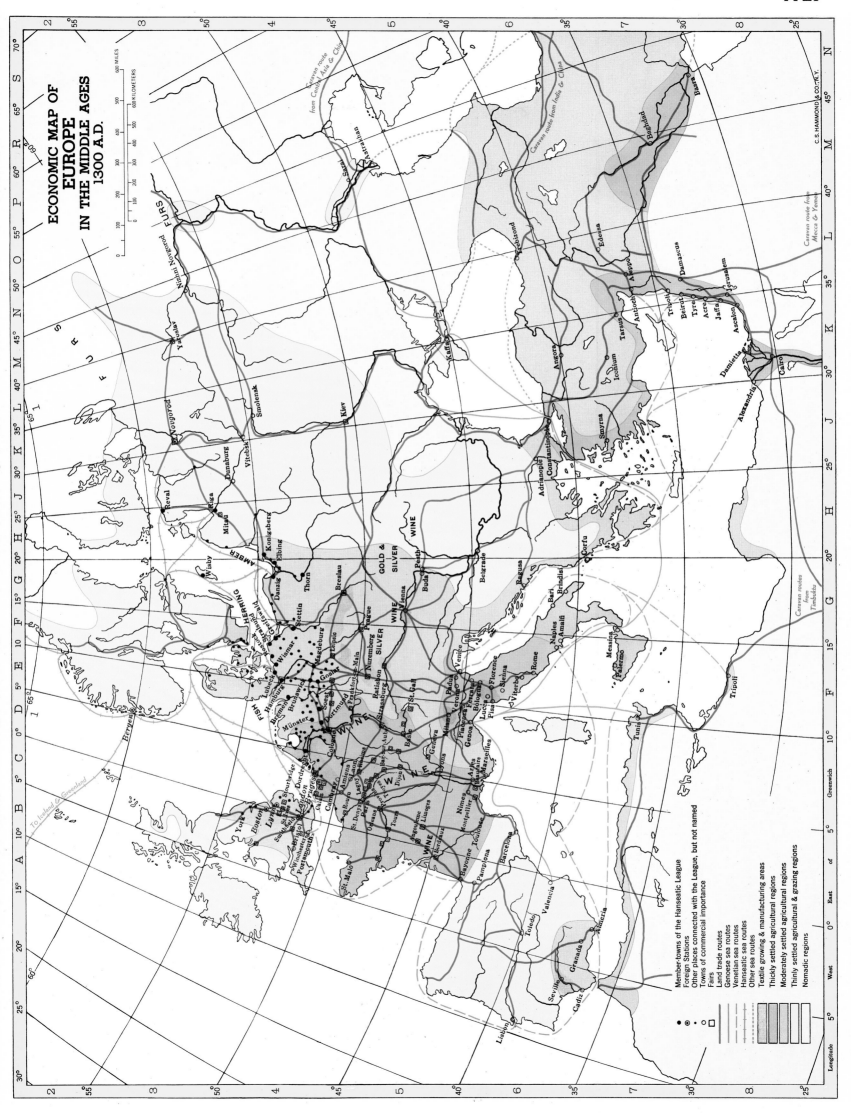

ECONOMIC MAP OF
EUROPE
IN THE MIDDLE AGES
1300 A.D.

600 MILES
600 KILOMETERS

C. S. HAMMOND & CO., N.Y.

Member-towns of the Hanseatic League
Foreign Stations
Other places connected with the League, but not named
Towns of commercial importance
Fairs
Land trade routes
Genoese sea routes
Venetian sea routes
Hanseatic sea routes
Other sea routes
Textile growing & manufacturing areas
Thickly settled agricultural regions
Moderately settled agricultural regions
Thinly settled agricultural & grazing regions
Nomadic regions

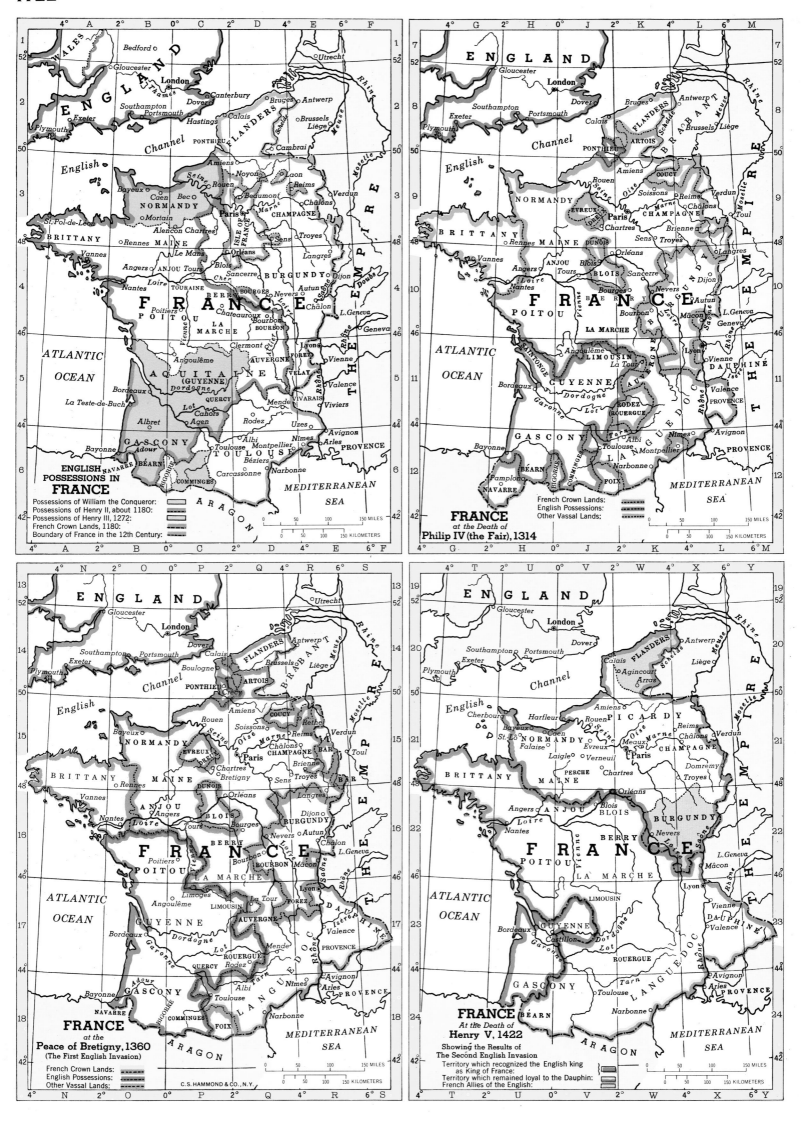

ENGLISH POSSESSIONS IN FRANCE

Possessions of William the Conqueror:
Possessions of Henry II, about 1180:
Possessions of Henry III, 1272:
French Crown Lands, 1180:
Boundary of France in the 12th Century:

FRANCE
at the Death of
Philip IV (the Fair), 1314

French Crown Lands:
English Possessions:
Other Vassal Lands:

FRANCE
at the
Peace of Bretigny, 1360
(The First English Invasion)

French Crown Lands:
English Possessions:
Other Vassal Lands:

C. S. HAMMOND & CO., N.Y.

FRANCE
At the Death of
Henry V, 1422

Showing the Results of
The Second English Invasion
Territory which recognized the English king
as King of France:
Territory which remained loyal to the Dauphin:
French Allies of the English:

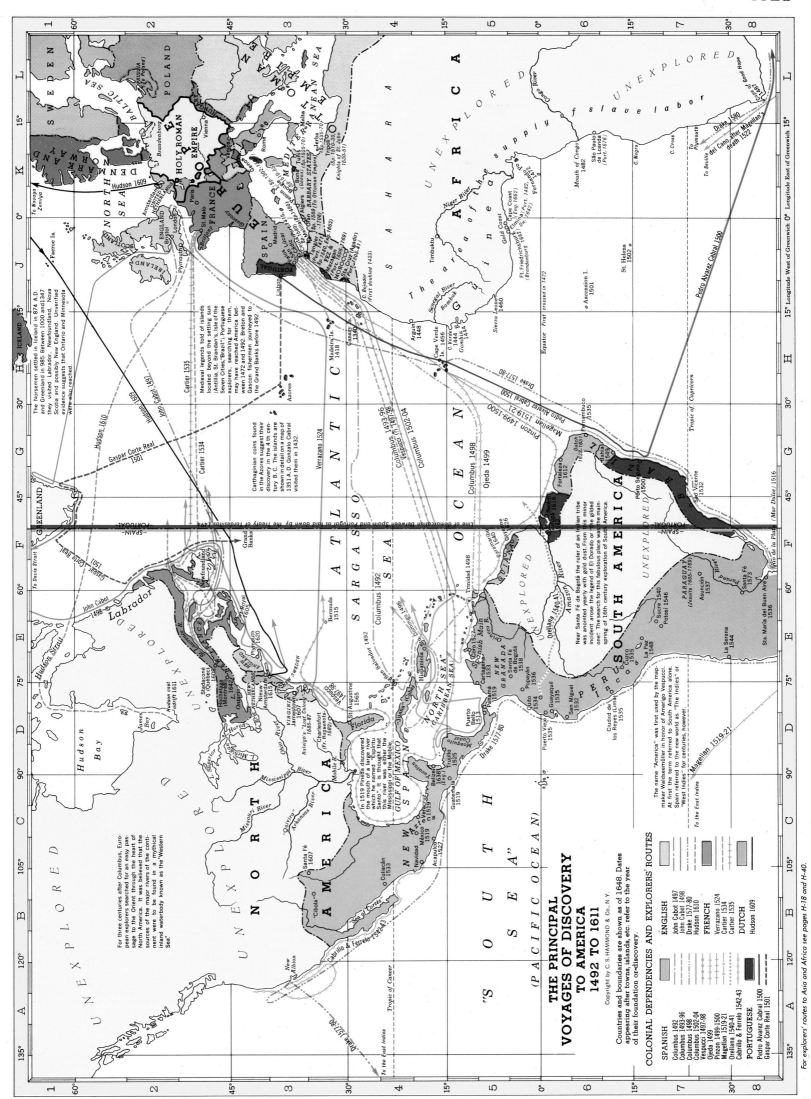

THE PRINCIPAL
VOYAGES OF DISCOVERY
TO AMERICA
1492 TO 1611

Copyright by C. S. HAMMOND & Co., N.Y.

Countries and boundaries are shown as of 1648. Dates appearing after towns, islands, etc. refer to the year of their foundation or discovery.

COLONIAL DEPENDENCIES AND EXPLORERS' ROUTES

SPANISH	ENGLISH
Columbus 1492	John Cabot 1497
Columbus 1493-96	John Cabot 1498
Columbus 1498	Drake 1577-80
Columbus 1502-04	Hudson 1610
Vespucci 1497-98	**FRENCH**
Ojeda 1499	Verrazano 1524
Pinzon 1499-1500	Cartier 1534
Magellan 1519/21	Cartier 1535
Orellana 1540/41	**DUTCH**
Cabrillo & Ferrelo 1542-43	Hudson 1609
PORTUGUESE	
Pedro Alvarez Cabral 1500	
Gaspar Corte Real 1501	

For explorers' routes to Asia and Africa see pages H-18 and H-40.

For three centuries after Columbus, European explorers searched for an easy passage to the Orient through the heart of North America. It was believed that the sources of the major rivers of the continent were to be found in a mythical inland waterbody known as the "Western Sea."

The Norsemen settled in Iceland in 874 A.D. and Greenland in 985. Between 1000 and 1347 they visited Labrador, Newfoundland, Nova Scotia and possibly New England. Unverified evidence suggests that Ontario and Minnesota were also reached.

Medieval legends told of islands located beyond the setting sun (Antilia, St. Brandan's, Isle of the Seven Cities, "Brazil"). Portuguese explorers, searching for them, may have reached America between 1472 and 1492. Breton and Gascon fishermen journeyed to the Grand Banks before 1492.

Carthaginian coins found in the Azores suggest their discovery in the 4th century B.C. The islands are shown in detail on a map of 1351 A.D. Gonzalo Cabral visited them in 1432.

In 1519 Pineda discovered the mouth of a large river which he named "Espiritu Santo." It is thought that this river was either the Mississippi or the Mobile.

Near Santa Fé de Bogotá the ruler of an Indian tribe was anointed yearly with gold dust. From this minor incident arose the legend of El Dorado or "the gilded one." The search for this fabulous place was the mainspring of 16th century exploration of South America.

The name "America" was first used by the mapmaker Waldseemüller in honor of Amerigo Vespucci. At first the term referred to South America alone. Spain referred to the new world as "The Indies" or "West Indies" for centuries, however.

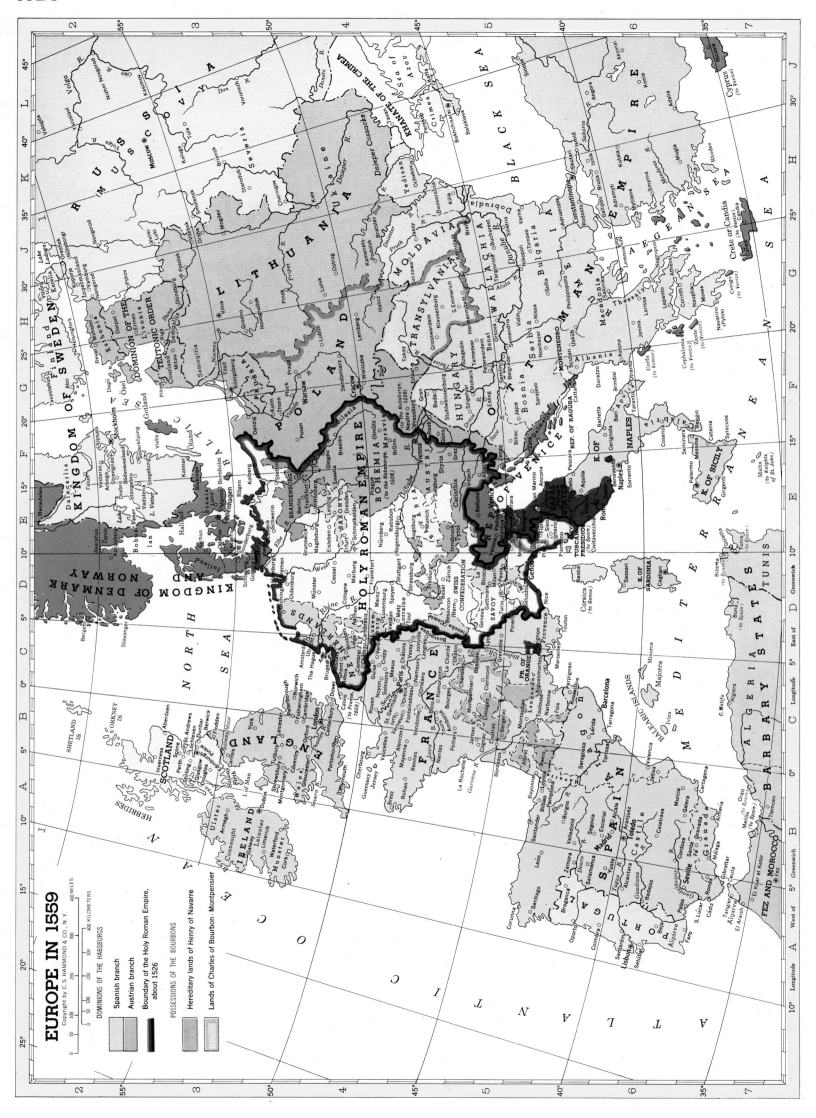

EUROPE IN 1559

Copyright by C. S. HAMMOND & CO., N.Y.

DOMINIONS OF THE HABSBURGS
Spanish branch
Austrian branch
Boundary of the Holy Roman Empire, about 1526

POSSESSIONS OF THE BOURBONS
Hereditary lands of Henry of Navarre
Lands of Charles of Bourbon-Montpensier

EUROPE IN 1648
AT THE PEACE OF WESTPHALIA

Copyright by C. S. HAMMOND & CO. N.Y.

Boundary of the Empire

Church Lands

Transylvania, independent of
Hungarian Kingdom with Turkish
Backing.

DOMINIONS OF THE HABSBURGS

Spanish Branch

Austrian Branch

400 MILES
300
200
100
50
0

400 KILOMETERS
300
200
100
50
0

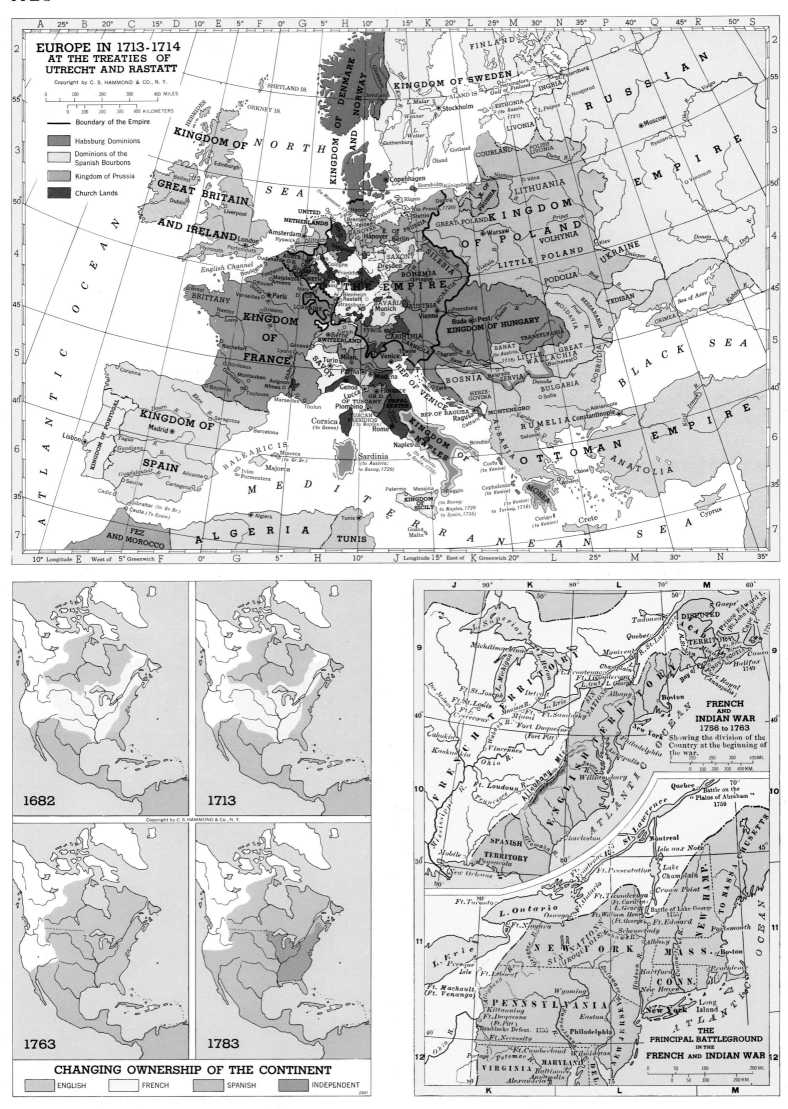

EUROPE IN 1713-1714 AT THE TREATIES OF UTRECHT AND RASTATT

Copyright by C. S. HAMMOND & CO., N.Y.

Boundary of the Empire

Habsburg Dominions
Dominions of the Spanish Bourbons
Kingdom of Prussia
Church Lands

CHANGING OWNERSHIP OF THE CONTINENT

1682   1713   1763   1783

Copyright by C. S. HAMMOND & CO., N.Y.

ENGLISH   FRENCH   SPANISH   INDEPENDENT

FRENCH AND INDIAN WAR 1756 to 1763

Showing the division of the Country at the beginning of the war.

Battle on the "Plains of Abraham" 1759

THE PRINCIPAL BATTLEGROUND IN THE FRENCH AND INDIAN WAR

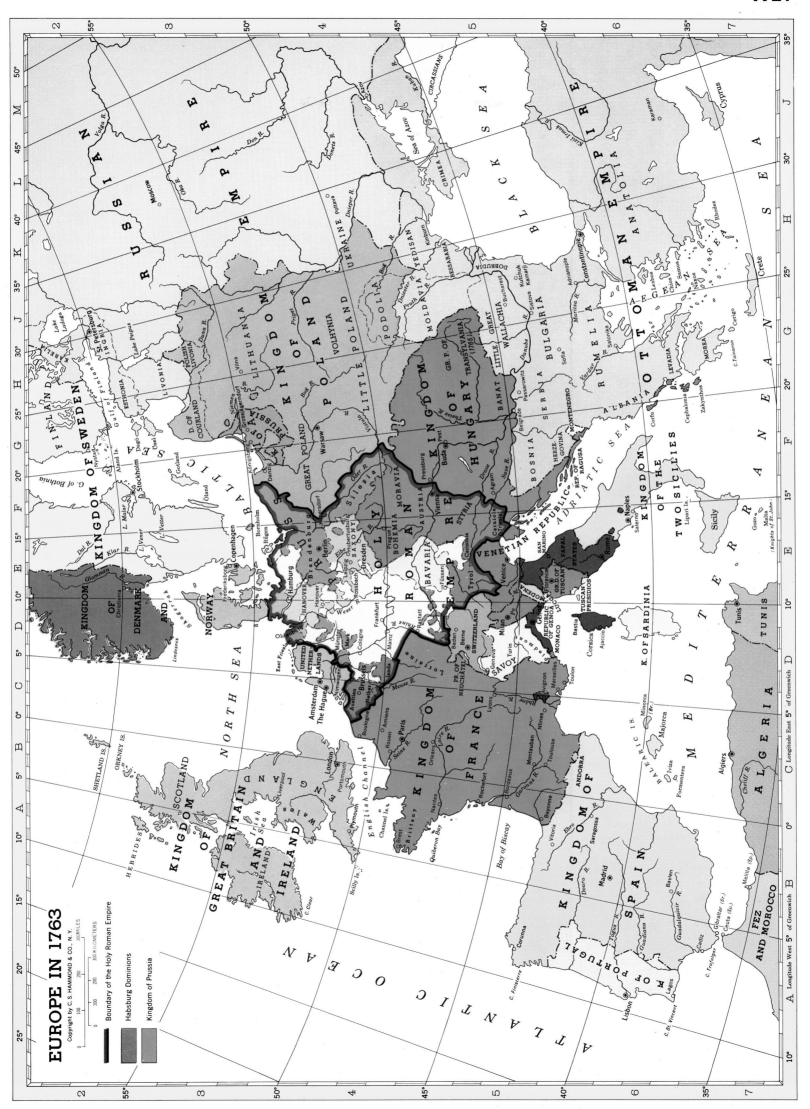

EUROPE IN 1763

Copyright by C.S. HAMMOND & CO., N.Y.

Boundary of the Holy Roman Empire

Habsburg Dominions

Kingdom of Prussia

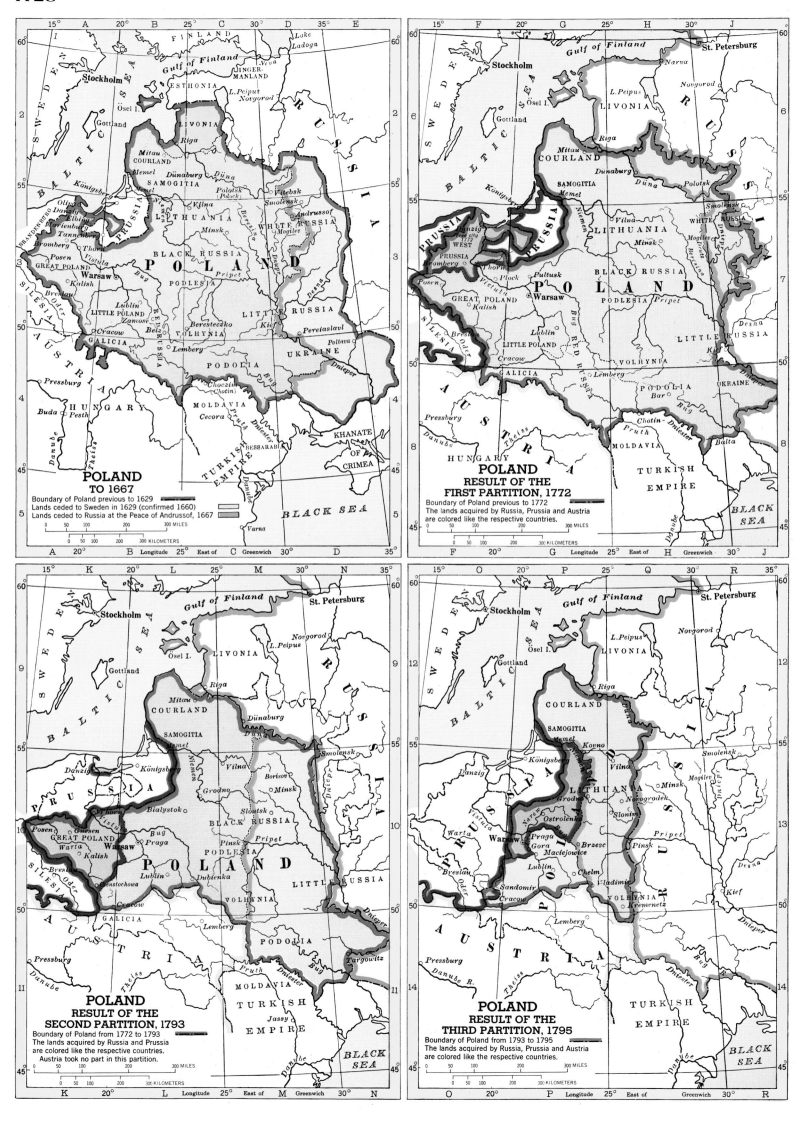

POLAND
TO 1667

Boundary of Poland previous to 1629
Lands ceded to Sweden in 1629 (confirmed 1660)
Lands ceded to Russia at the Peace of Andrussof, 1667

POLAND
RESULT OF THE
FIRST PARTITION, 1772

Boundary of Poland previous to 1772
The lands acquired by Russia, Prussia and Austria
are colored like the respective countries.

POLAND
RESULT OF THE
SECOND PARTITION, 1793

Boundary of Poland from 1772 to 1793
The lands acquired by Russia and Prussia
are colored like the respective countries.
Austria took no part in this partition.

POLAND
RESULT OF THE
THIRD PARTITION, 1795

Boundary of Poland from 1793 to 1795
The lands acquired by Russia, Prussia and Austria
are colored like the respective countries.

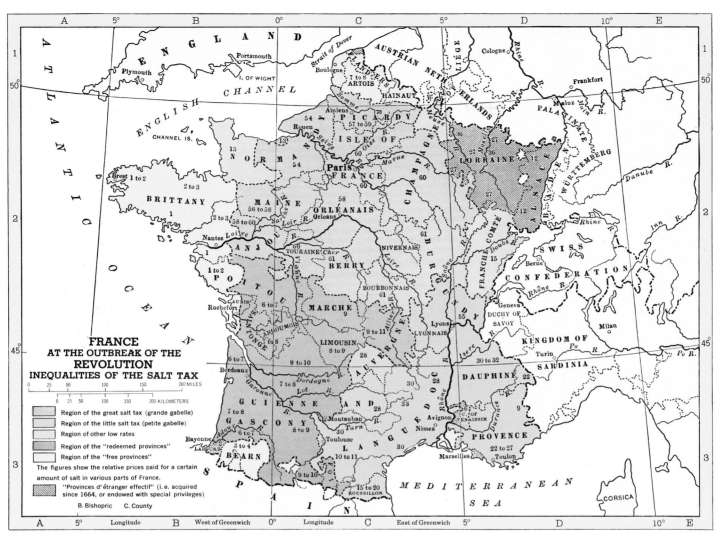

FRANCE
AT THE OUTBREAK OF THE
REVOLUTION
INEQUALITIES OF THE SALT TAX

Region of the great salt tax (grande gabelle)
Region of the little salt tax (petite gabelle)
Region of other low rates
Region of the "redeemed provinces"
Region of the "free provinces"

The figures show the relative prices paid for a certain amount of salt in various parts of France.

"Provinces d'étranger effectif" (i. e. acquired since 1664, or endowed with special privileges)

B. Bishopric   C. County

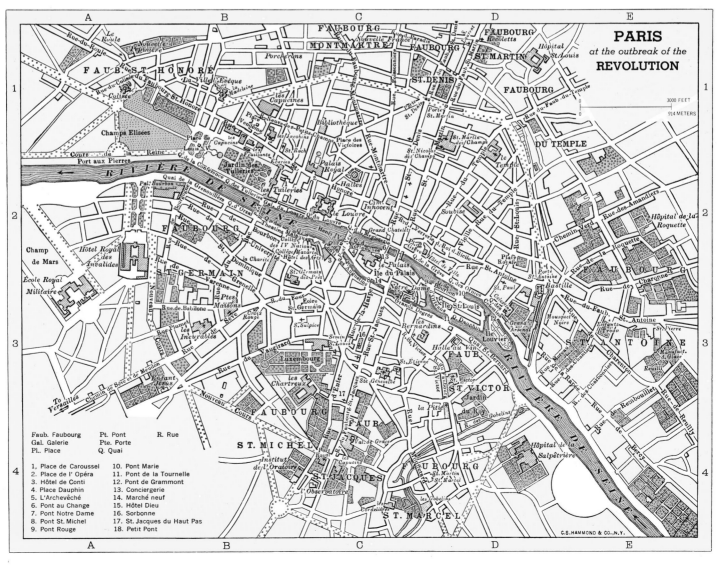

PARIS
at the outbreak of the
REVOLUTION

Faub. Faubourg   Pt. Pont   R. Rue
Gal. Galerie   Pte. Porte   Q. Quai
Pl. Place

1. Place de Caroussel   10. Pont Marie
2. Place de l' Opéra   11. Pont de la Tournelle
3. Hôtel de Conti   12. Pont de Grammont
4. Place Dauphin   13. Conciergerie
5. L'Archevêché   14. Marché neuf
6. Pont au Change   15. Hôtel Dieu
7. Pont Notre Dame   16. Sorbonne
8. Pont St. Michel   17. St. Jacques du Haut Pas
9. Pont Rouge   18. Petit Pont

C.S. HAMMOND & CO., N.Y.

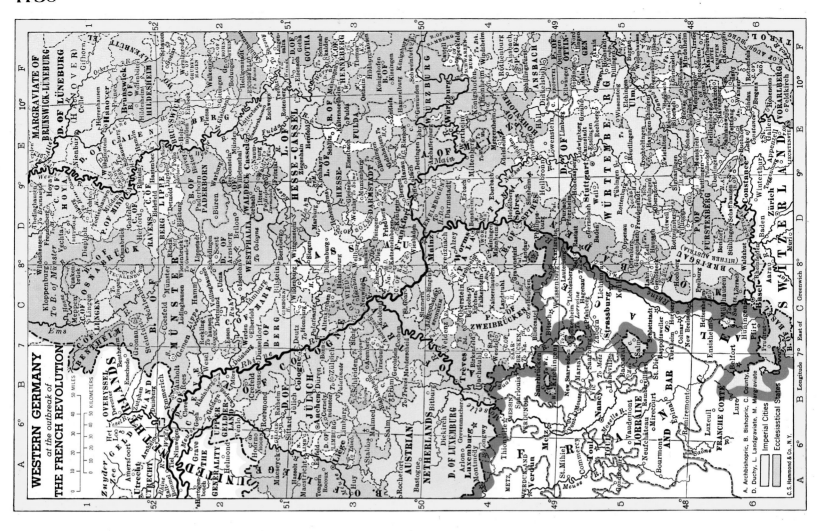

WESTERN GERMANY
at the outbreak of
THE FRENCH REVOLUTION

A. Archbishopric, B. Bishopric, C. County,
D. Duchy, L. Landgraviate, M. Margraviate

Imperial Cities

Ecclesiastical States

C. S. Hammond & Co., N.Y.

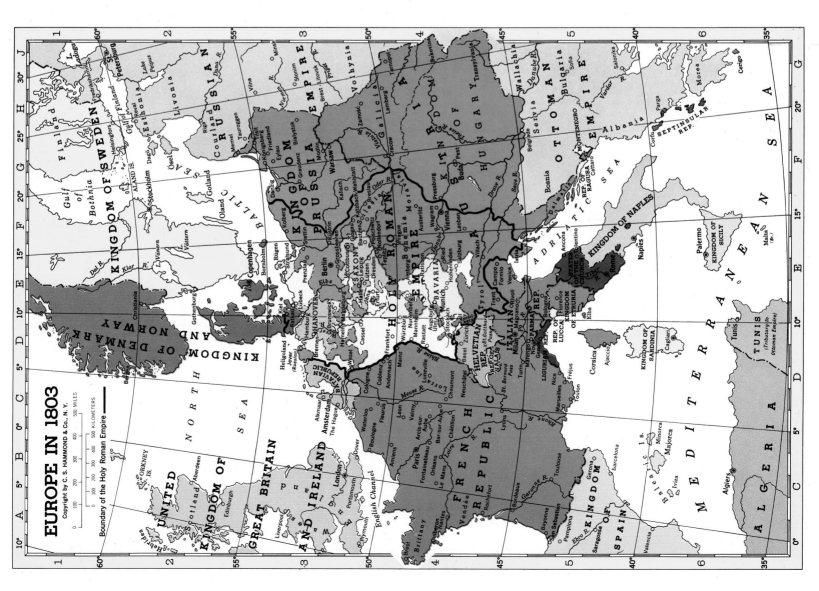

EUROPE IN 1803

Copyright by C. S. Hammond & Co., N.Y.

—————— Boundary of the Holy Roman Empire

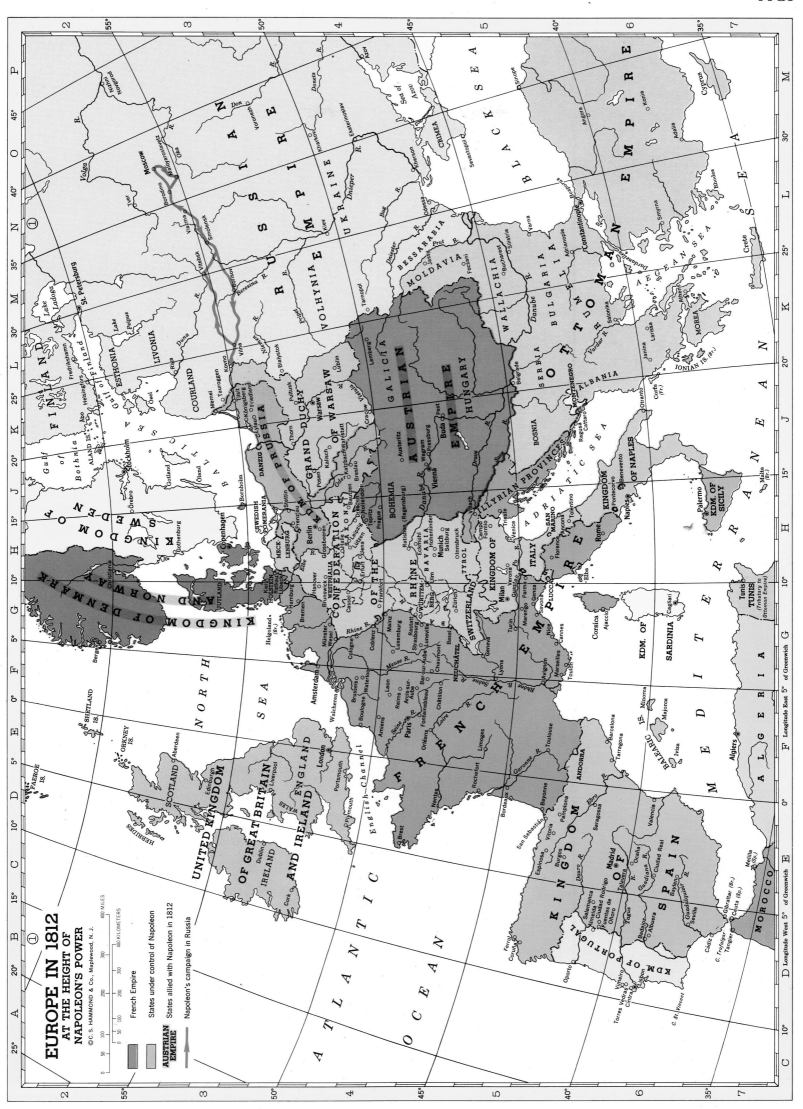

EUROPE IN 1812
AT THE HEIGHT OF
NAPOLEON'S POWER

©C. S. HAMMOND & Co., Maplewood, N. J.

French Empire
States under control of Napoleon
States allied with Napoleon in 1812
Napoleon's campaign in Russia

AUSTRIAN EMPIRE

MILES
0   50   100   200   300   400
0   50   100   200   300   400
KILOMETERS

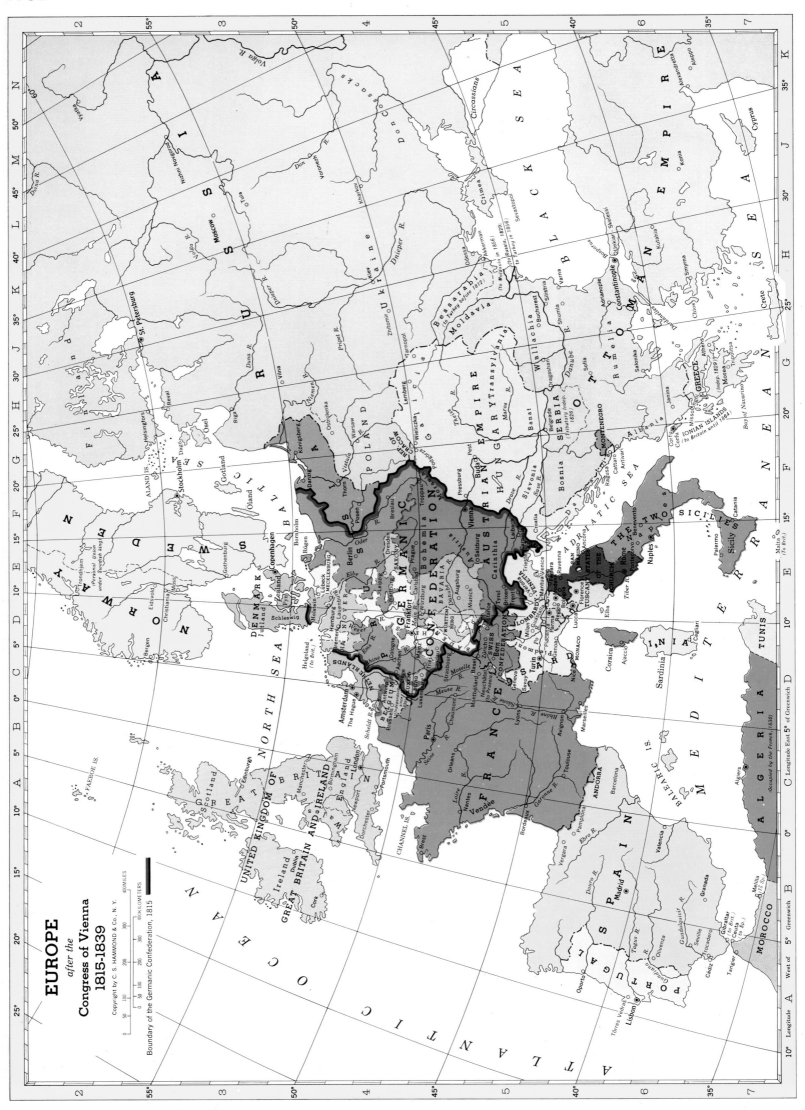

EUROPE
after the
Congress of Vienna
1815-1839

Copyright by C. S. HAMMOND & Co. N. Y.

Boundary of the Germanic Confederation, 1815

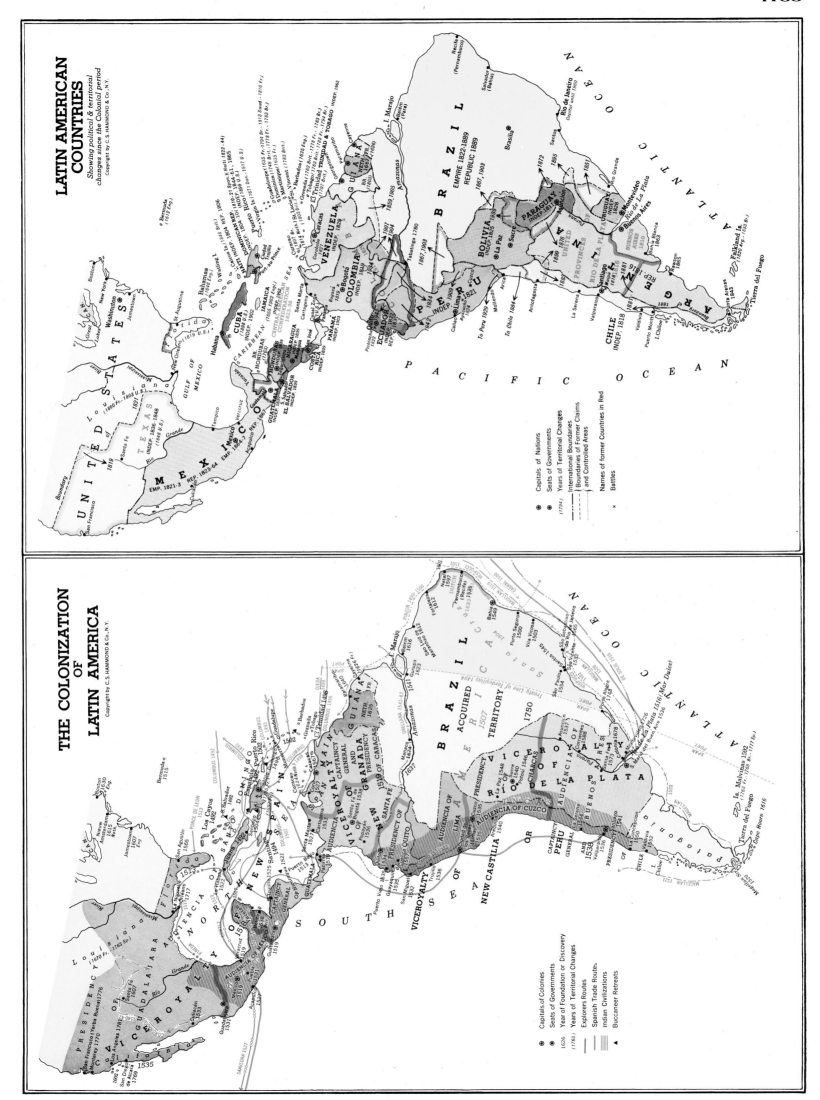

LATIN AMERICAN COUNTRIES

Showing political & territorial changes since the Colonial period

Copyright by C.S. HAMMOND & Co. N.Y.

THE COLONIZATION OF LATIN AMERICA

Copyright by C.S. HAMMOND & Co. N.Y.

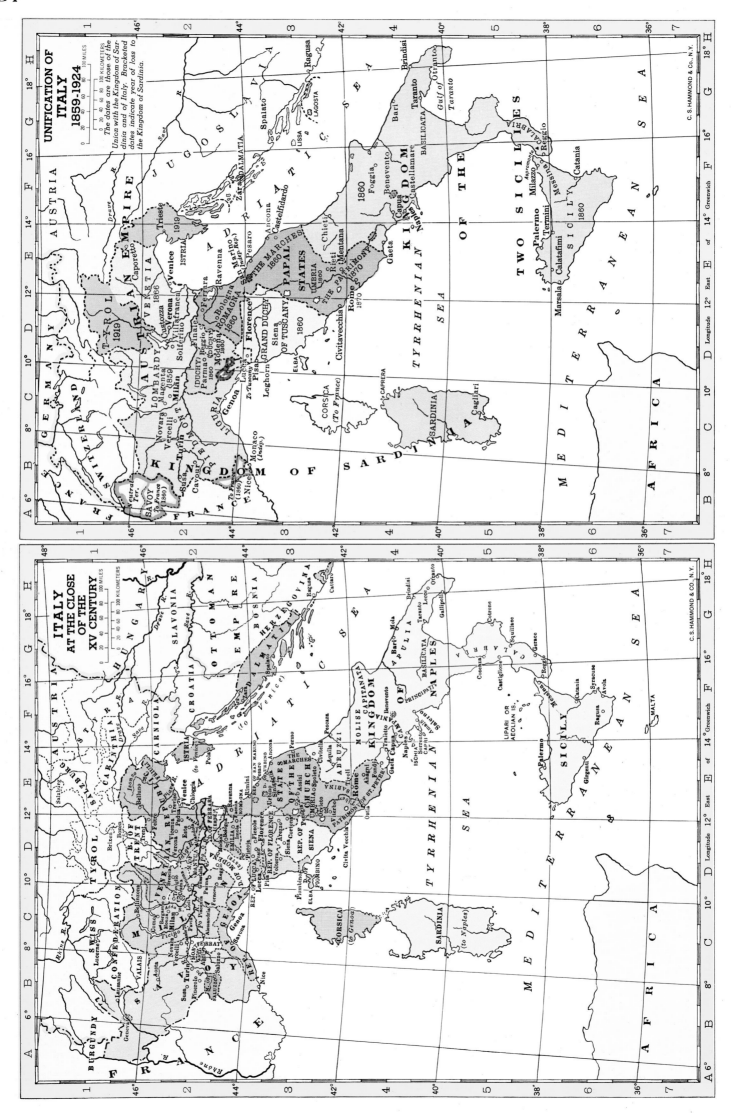

UNIFICATION OF ITALY
1859-1924

The dates are those of the Union with the Kingdom of Sardinia and of Italy. Bracketed dates indicate year of loss to the Kingdom of Sardinia.

C. S. HAMMOND & Co., N.Y.

ITALY AT THE CLOSE OF THE XV CENTURY

C. S. HAMMOND & Co., N.Y.

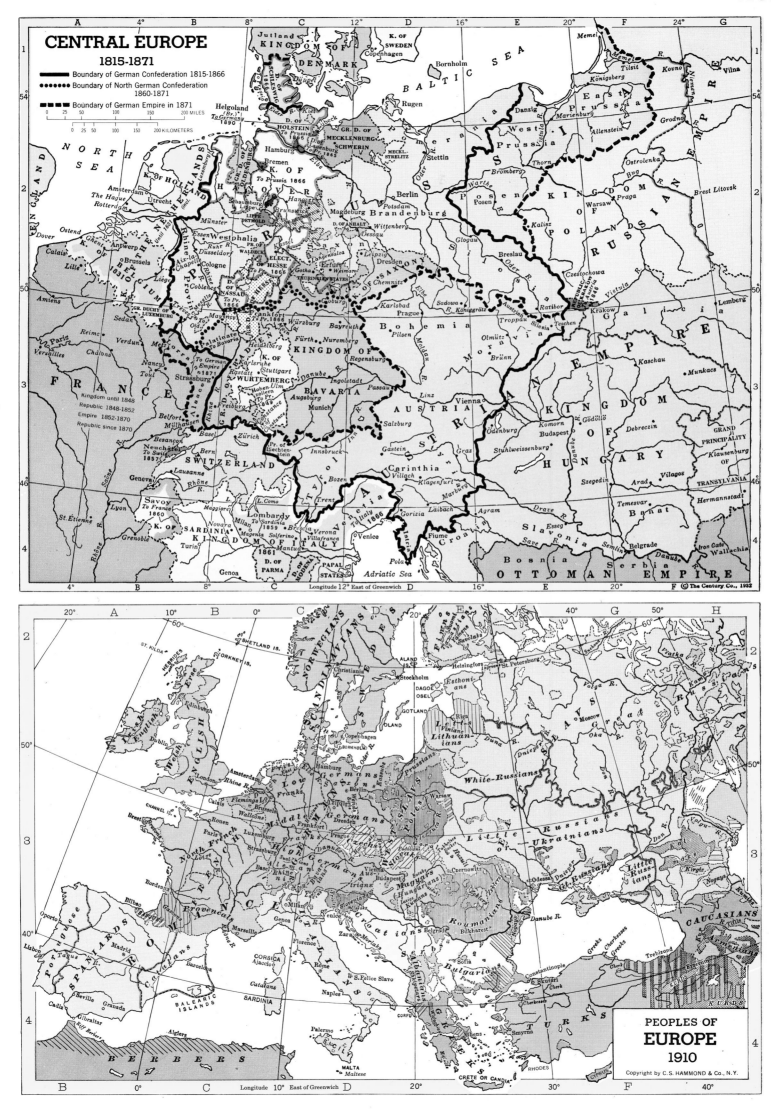

CENTRAL EUROPE
1815-1871

Boundary of German Confederation 1815-1866
Boundary of North German Confederation 1860-1871
Boundary of German Empire in 1871

PEOPLES OF EUROPE 1910

Copyright by C.S. HAMMOND & Co., N.Y.

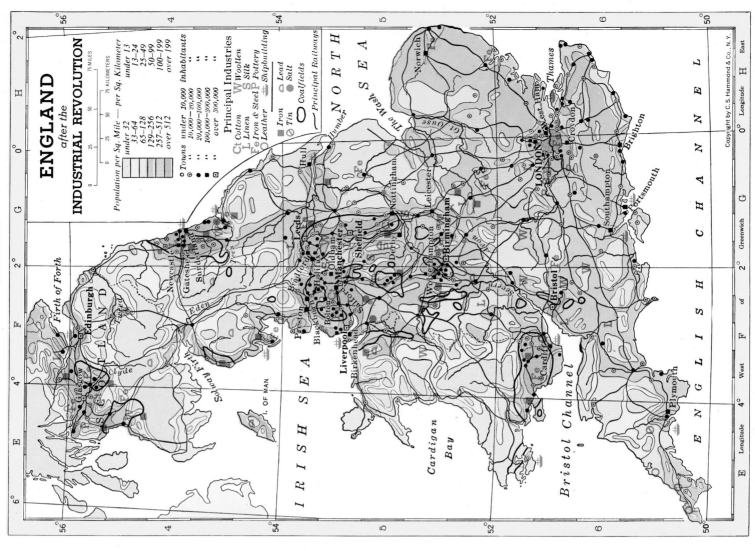

ENGLAND
after the
INDUSTRIAL REVOLUTION

Population per Sq. Mile — per Sq. Kilometer

	under 32	under 13
	33–64	13–24
	65–128	25–49
	129–256	50–99
	257–512	100–199
	over 512	over 199

Towns under 10,000 inhabitants
10,000–20,000
20,000–100,000
100,000–300,000
over 300,000

Principal Industries
Ct Cotton   W Woollen
L Linen   S Silk
Fe Iron & Steel   P Pottery
Leather   Shipbuilding

Iron   Lead
Tin   Salt
Coalfields
Principal Railways

Copyright by C. S. Hammond & Co., N. Y.

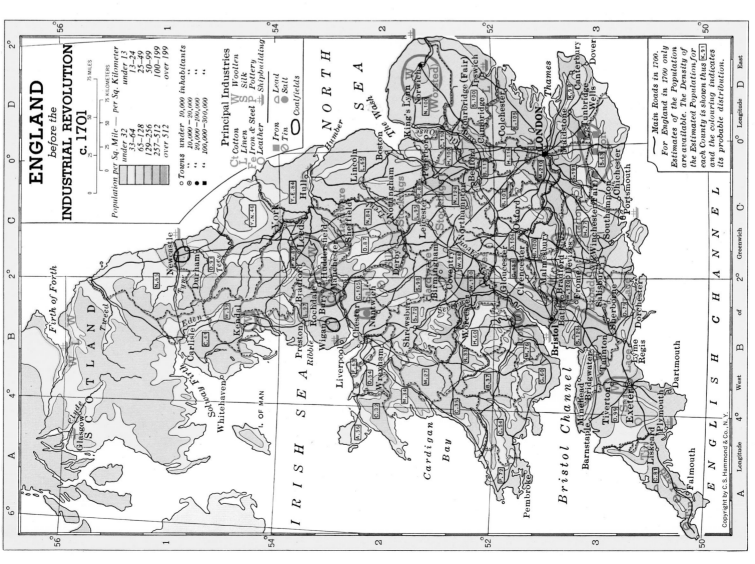

ENGLAND
before the
INDUSTRIAL REVOLUTION
c. 1701

Population per Sq. Mile — per Sq. Kilometer

	under 32	under 13
	33–64	13–24
	65–128	25–49
	129–256	50–99
	257–512	100–199
	over 512	over 199

Towns under 10,000 inhabitants
10,000–20,000
20,000–100,000
100,000–300,000
over 300,000

Principal Industries
Ct Cotton   W Woollen
L Linen   S Silk
Fe Iron & Steel   P Pottery
Leather   Shipbuilding

Iron   Lead
Tin   Salt
Coalfields

Main Roads in 1700.
For England in 1700 only
Estimates of the Population
are available. The Density of
the Estimated Population for
each County is shown thus [K.91]
and the colouring indicates
its probable distribution.

Copyright by C. S. Hammond & Co., N. Y.

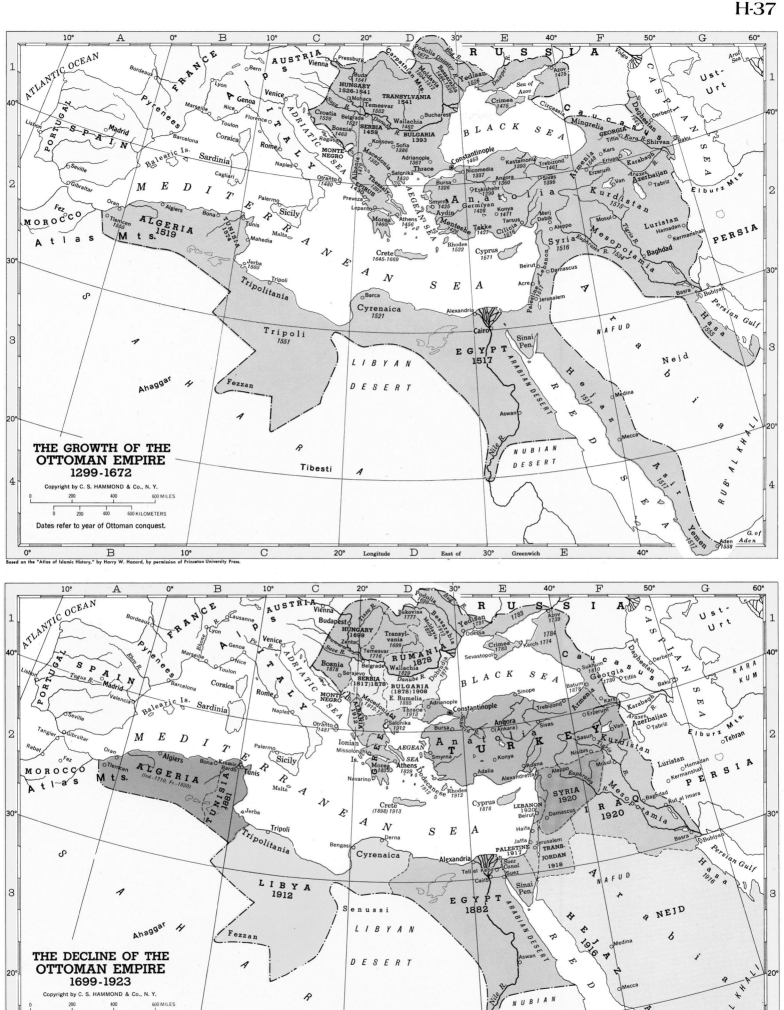

THE GROWTH OF THE
OTTOMAN EMPIRE
1299-1672

Copyright by C. S. HAMMOND & Co., N. Y.

Dates refer to year of Ottoman conquest.

Based on the "Atlas of Islamic History," by Harry W. Hazard, by permission of Princeton University Press.

THE DECLINE OF THE
OTTOMAN EMPIRE
1699-1923

Copyright by C. S. HAMMOND & Co., N. Y.

Areas taken by Russia
Areas taken by Britain
Areas taken by France
Areas taken by Italy
Areas taken by Austria

Dates refer to year of Ottoman loss.

Based on the "Atlas of Islamic History," by Harry W. Hazard, by permission of Princeton University Press.

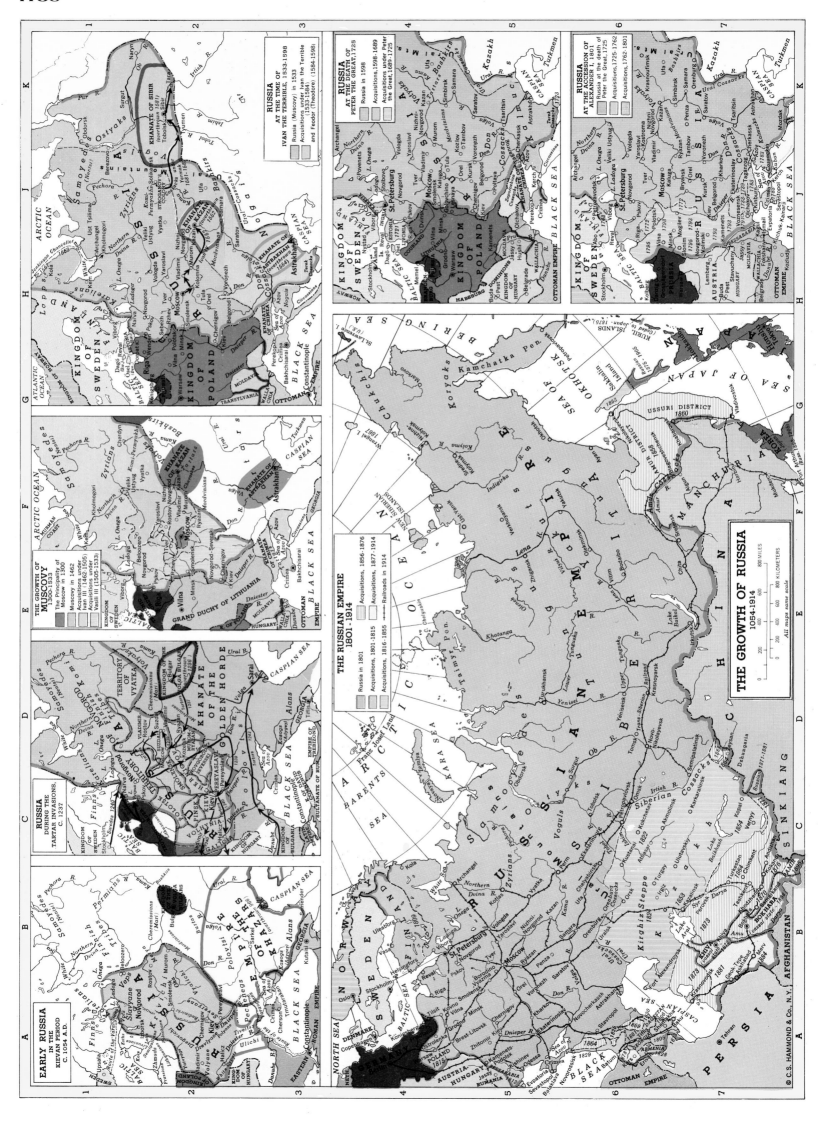

RUSSIA AT THE TIME OF IVAN THE TERRIBLE, 1533-1598
Russia (Muscovy) in 1533
Acquisitions under Ivan the Terrible (1533-1584) and Feodor (Theodore) (1584-1598)

RUSSIA AT THE DEATH OF PETER THE GREAT, 1725
Russia in 1598
Acquisitions, 1598-1689
Acquisitions under Peter the Great, 1689-1725

RUSSIA AT THE ACCESSION OF ALEXANDER I, 1801
Russia at the death of Peter the Great, 1725
Acquisitions, 1725-1762
Acquisitions, 1762-1801

THE GROWTH OF MUSCOVY 1300-1533
The Principality of Moscow in 1300
Muscovy in 1462
Acquisitions under Ivan III (1462-1505)
Acquisitions under Vasili III (1505-1533)

RUSSIA DURING THE TARTAR INVASIONS, C. 1237

THE RUSSIAN EMPIRE 1801-1914
Russia in 1801
Acquisitions, 1801-1815
Acquisitions, 1816-1855
Acquisitions, 1856-1876
Acquisitions, 1877-1914
Railroads in 1914

EARLY RUSSIA IN THE KIEVAN PERIOD C. 1054 A.D.

THE GROWTH OF RUSSIA 1054-1914

©C.S. HAMMOND & Co., N.Y.

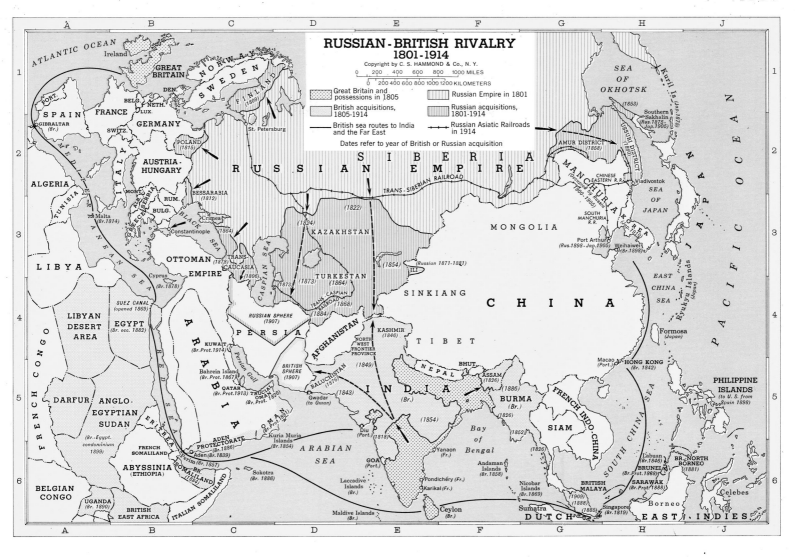

RUSSIAN-BRITISH RIVALRY
1801-1914
Copyright by C. S. HAMMOND & Co., N.Y.

0   200   400   600   800   1000 MILES
0 200 400 600 800 1000 1200 KILOMETERS

Great Britain and possessions in 1805

British acquisitions, 1805-1914

British sea routes to India and the Far East

Russian Empire in 1801

Russian acquisitions, 1801-1914

Russian Asiatic Railroads in 1914

Dates refer to year of British or Russian acquisition

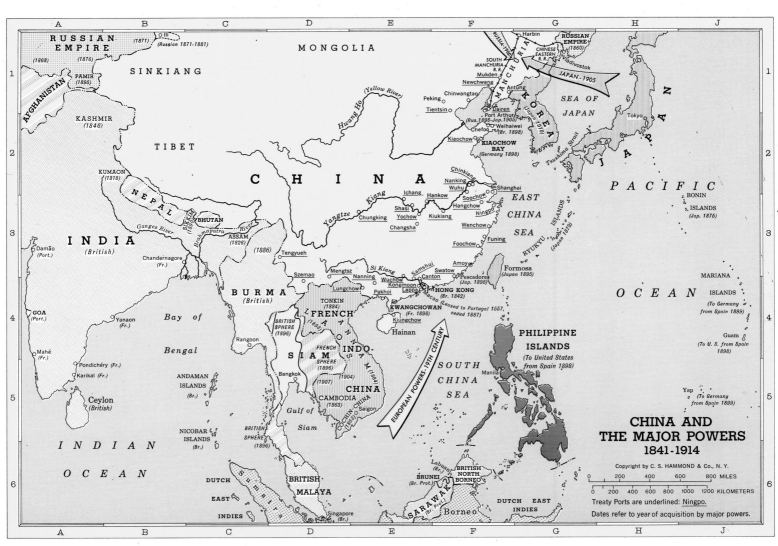

CHINA AND
THE MAJOR POWERS
1841-1914
Copyright by C. S. HAMMOND & Co., N.Y.

0   200   400   600   800 MILES
0 200 400 600 800 1000 1200 KILOMETERS

Treaty Ports are underlined: Ningpo.

Dates refer to year of acquisition by major powers.

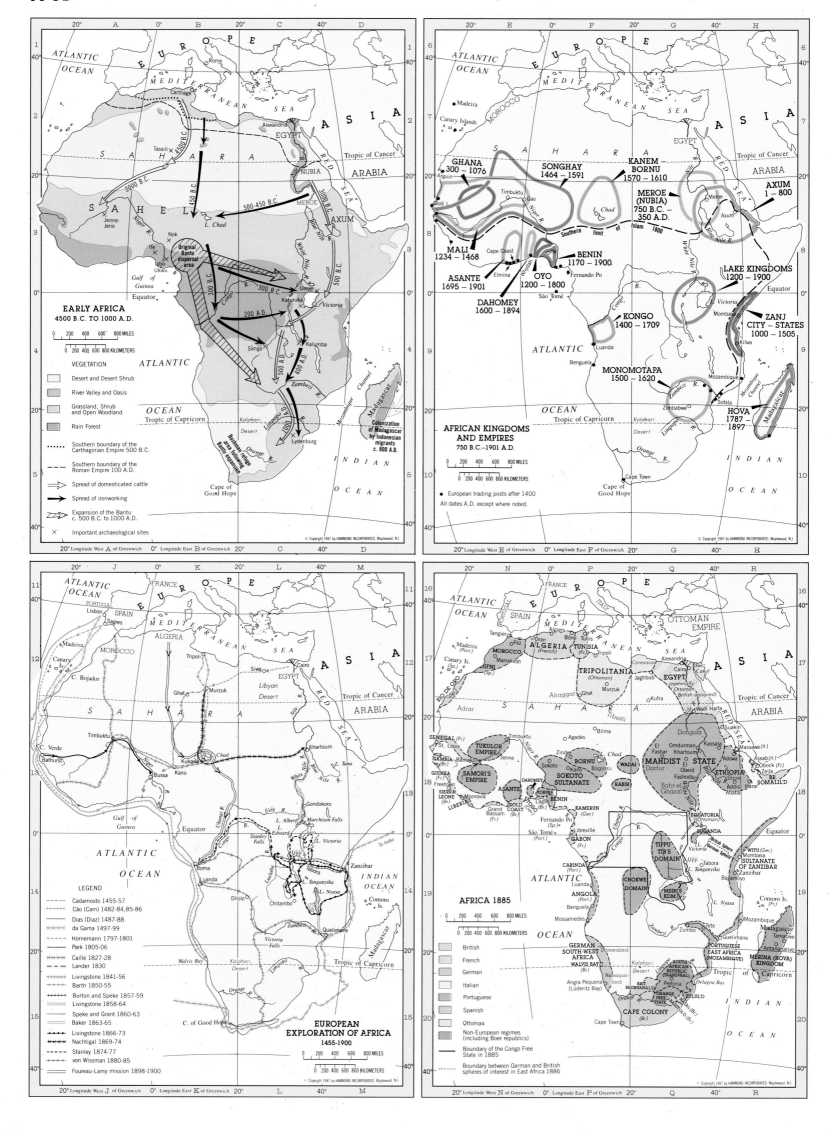

EARLY AFRICA
4500 B.C. TO 1000 A.D.

VEGETATION

Desert and Desert Shrub

River Valley and Oasis

Grassland, Shrub and Open Woodland

Rain Forest

········· Southern boundary of the Carthaginian Empire 500 B.C.

– – – Southern boundary of the Roman Empire 100 A.D.

⇨ Spread of domesticated cattle

➜ Spread of ironworking

⇨ Expansion of the Bantu c. 500 B.C. to 1000 A.D.

× Important archaeological sites

© Copyright 1987 by HAMMOND INCORPORATED, Maplewood, N.J.

AFRICAN KINGDOMS AND EMPIRES
750 B.C.–1901 A.D.

● European trading posts after 1400

All dates A.D. except where noted.

© Copyright 1987 by HAMMOND INCORPORATED, Maplewood, N.J.

GHANA 300 – 1076
SONGHAY 1464 – 1591
KANEM – BORNU 1570 – 1610
MEROE (NUBIA) 750 B.C. – 350 A.D.
AXUM 1 – 800
MALI 1234 – 1468
BENIN 1170 – 1900
LAKE KINGDOMS 1200 – 1900
ASANTE 1695 – 1901
OYO 1200 – 1800
ZANJ CITY – STATES 1000 – 1505
DAHOMEY 1600 – 1894
KONGO 1400 – 1709
MONOMOTAPA 1500 – 1620
HOVA 1787 – 1897

EUROPEAN EXPLORATION OF AFRICA
1455-1900

LEGEND

– – – Cadamosto 1455-57
+++++ Cão (Cam) 1482-84, 85-86
——— Dias (Diaz) 1487-88
——— da Gama 1497-99
– – – Hornemann 1797-1801
——— Park 1805-06
×××× Caillé 1827-28
– – – Lander 1830
+++++ Livingstone 1841-56
——— Barth 1850-55
+++++ Burton and Speke 1857-59
——— Livingstone 1858-64
——— Speke and Grant 1860-63
——— Baker 1863-65
+++++ Livingstone 1866-73
×××× Nachtigal 1869-74
——— Stanley 1874-77
+++++ von Wissman 1880-85
——— Foureau-Lamy mission 1898-1900

© Copyright 1987 by HAMMOND INCORPORATED, Maplewood, N.J.

AFRICA 1885

British
French
German
Italian
Portuguese
Spanish
Ottoman
Non-European regimes (including Boer republics)

——— Boundary of the Congo Free State in 1885

– – – Boundary between German and British spheres of interest in East Africa 1886

© Copyright 1987 by HAMMOND INCORPORATED, Maplewood, N.J.

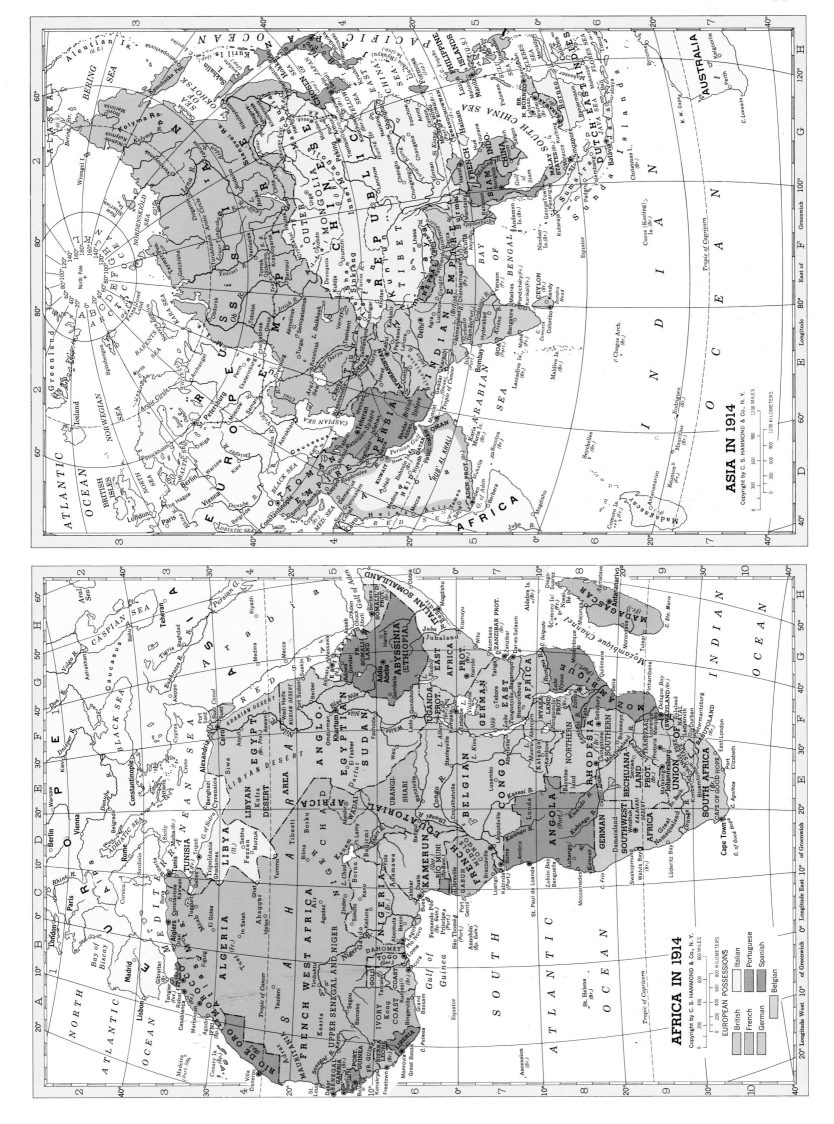

ASIA IN 1914

Copyright by C. S. HAMMOND & Co., N.Y.

AFRICA IN 1914

Copyright by C. S. HAMMOND & Co., N.Y.

EUROPEAN POSSESSIONS

British
French
German
Italian
Portuguese
Spanish
Belgian

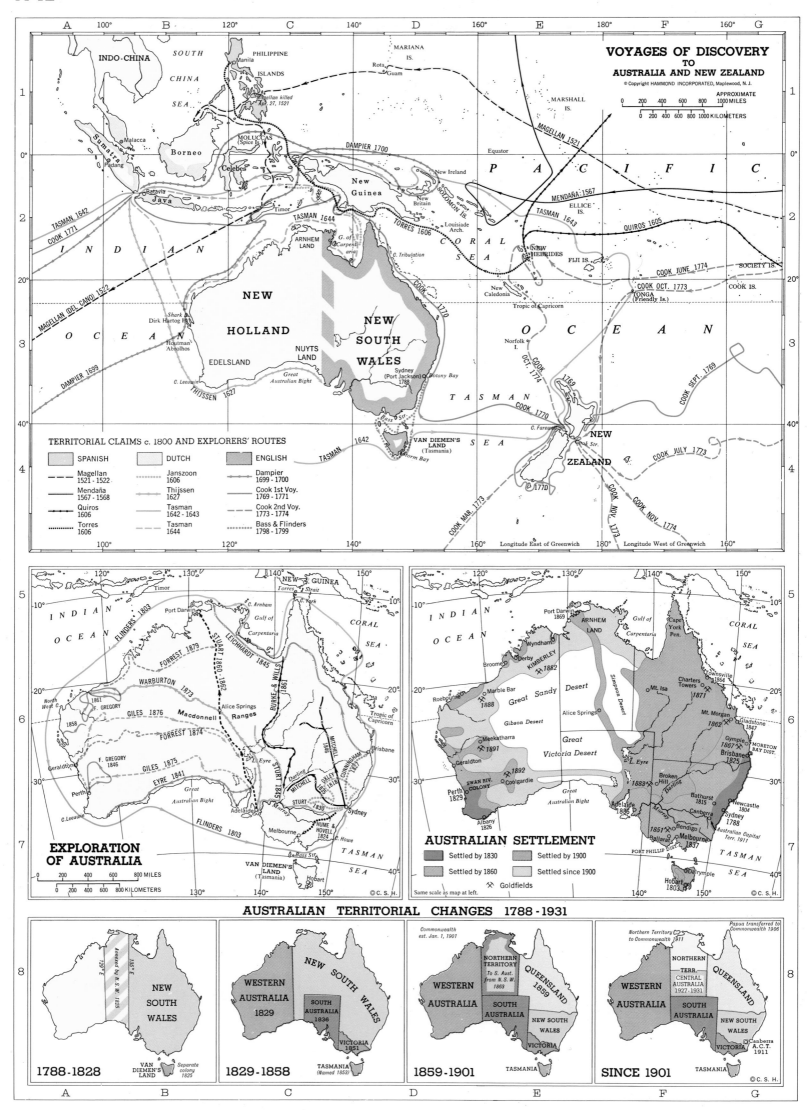

VOYAGES OF DISCOVERY
TO
AUSTRALIA AND NEW ZEALAND
© Copyright HAMMOND INCORPORATED, Maplewood, N.J.

APPROXIMATE MILES
0 200 400 600 800 1000 MILES
0 200 400 600 800 1000 KILOMETERS

TERRITORIAL CLAIMS c. 1800 AND EXPLORERS' ROUTES

SPANISH   DUTCH   ENGLISH

Magellan 1521-1522
Mendaña 1567-1568
Quiros 1606
Torres 1606
Janszoon 1606
Thijssen 1627
Tasman 1642-1643
Tasman 1644
Dampier 1699-1700
Cook 1st Voy. 1769-1771
Cook 2nd Voy. 1773-1774
Bass & Flinders 1798-1799

Longitude East of Greenwich   Longitude West of Greenwich

EXPLORATION OF AUSTRALIA

200 400 600 800 MILES
200 400 600 800 KILOMETERS

AUSTRALIAN SETTLEMENT

Settled by 1830
Settled by 1860
Settled by 1900
Settled since 1900
Goldfields

Same scale as map at left.

AUSTRALIAN TERRITORIAL CHANGES 1788-1931

1788-1828
NEW SOUTH WALES
Annexed by N.S.W. 1825
129° E   135° E
VAN DIEMEN'S LAND
Separate colony 1825

1829-1858
WESTERN AUSTRALIA 1829
SOUTH AUSTRALIA 1836
NEW SOUTH WALES
VICTORIA 1851
TASMANIA (Named 1853)

1859-1901
Commonwealth est. Jan. 1, 1901
WESTERN AUSTRALIA
NORTHERN TERRITORY To S. Aust. from 1863
QUEENSLAND 1859
SOUTH AUSTRALIA
NEW SOUTH WALES
VICTORIA
TASMANIA

SINCE 1901
Northern Territory to Commonwealth 1911
Papua transferred to Commonwealth 1906
WESTERN AUSTRALIA
NORTHERN TERR.
CENTRAL AUSTRALIA 1927-1931
QUEENSLAND
SOUTH AUSTRALIA
NEW SOUTH WALES
VICTORIA
Canberra A.C.T. 1911
TASMANIA

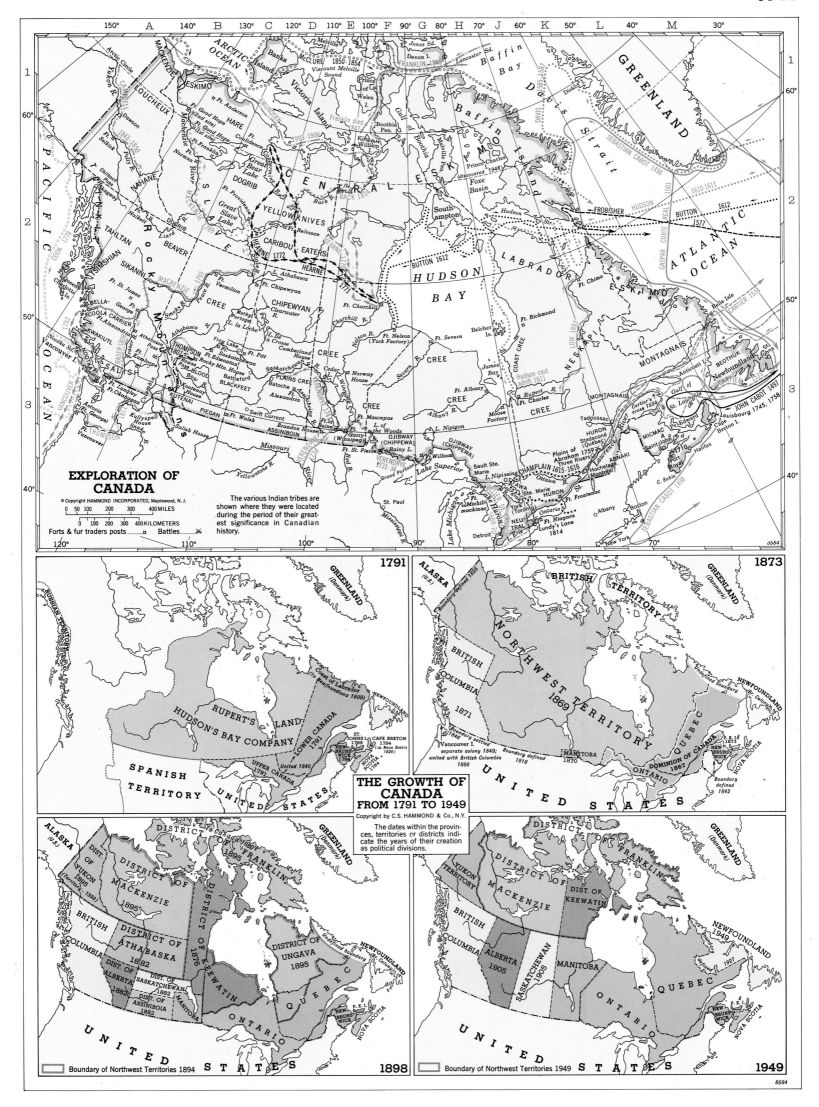

EXPLORATION OF CANADA

© Copyright HAMMOND INCORPORATED, Maplewood, N.J.

0 50 100 200 300 400 MILES

0 100 200 300 400 KILOMETERS

Forts & fur traders posts ——— Battles ✕

The various Indian tribes are shown where they were located during the period of their greatest significance in Canadian history.

1791

1873

THE GROWTH OF CANADA
FROM 1791 TO 1949

Copyright by C.S. HAMMOND & Co., N.Y.

The dates within the provinces, territories or districts indicate the years of their creation as political divisions.

Boundary of Northwest Territories 1894

1898

Boundary of Northwest Territories 1949

1949

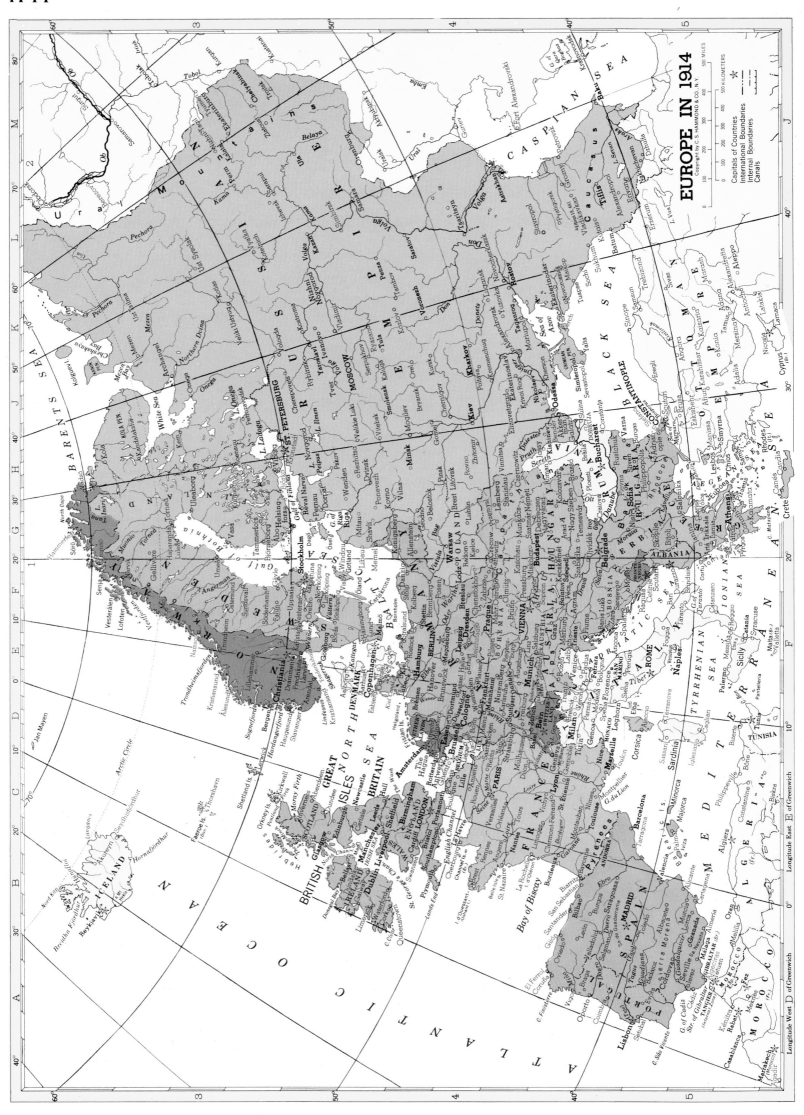

EUROPE IN 1914

Copyright by C. S. HAMMOND & CO., N.Y.

Capitals of Countries ⋆
International Boundaries
Internal Boundaries
Canals

EUROPE AND THE NEAR EAST

500 MILES
500 KILOMETERS

– – – Stabilized Line on the Western Front, 1914-1917

– – – Eastern Front on the Eve of the Russian Revolution, Oct. 1917

······ Limit of Allied Advances in the East

Area Occupied by the Central Powers after Brest Litovsk Treaty, 1918

THE FIRST WORLD WAR
1914-1918

© C. S. HAMMOND & Co., Maplewood, N. J.

The Allies

Neutral States

Advances of the Allies

The Central Powers

Areas Occupied by the Central Powers

Advances of the Central Powers

THE WESTERN FRONT

80 MILES
80 KILOMETERS

Limit of German Advance, 1914

Limit of Trench Warfare, 1914-1917

Hindenburg Line, 1917

Limit of Final German Advance, 1918

Armistice Line, November 11, 1918

Limit of Allied Occupation Zone

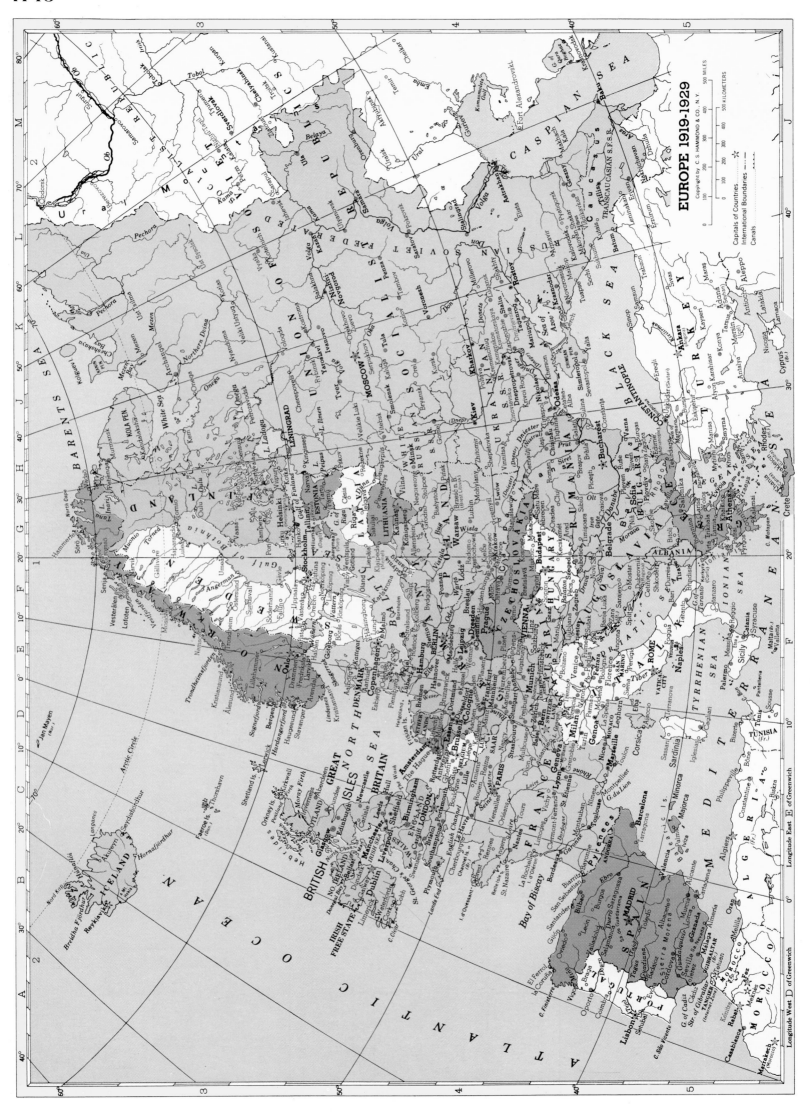

EUROPE 1919-1929

Copyright by C. S. HAMMOND & CO., N.Y.

Capitals of Countries ★
International Boundaries
Canals

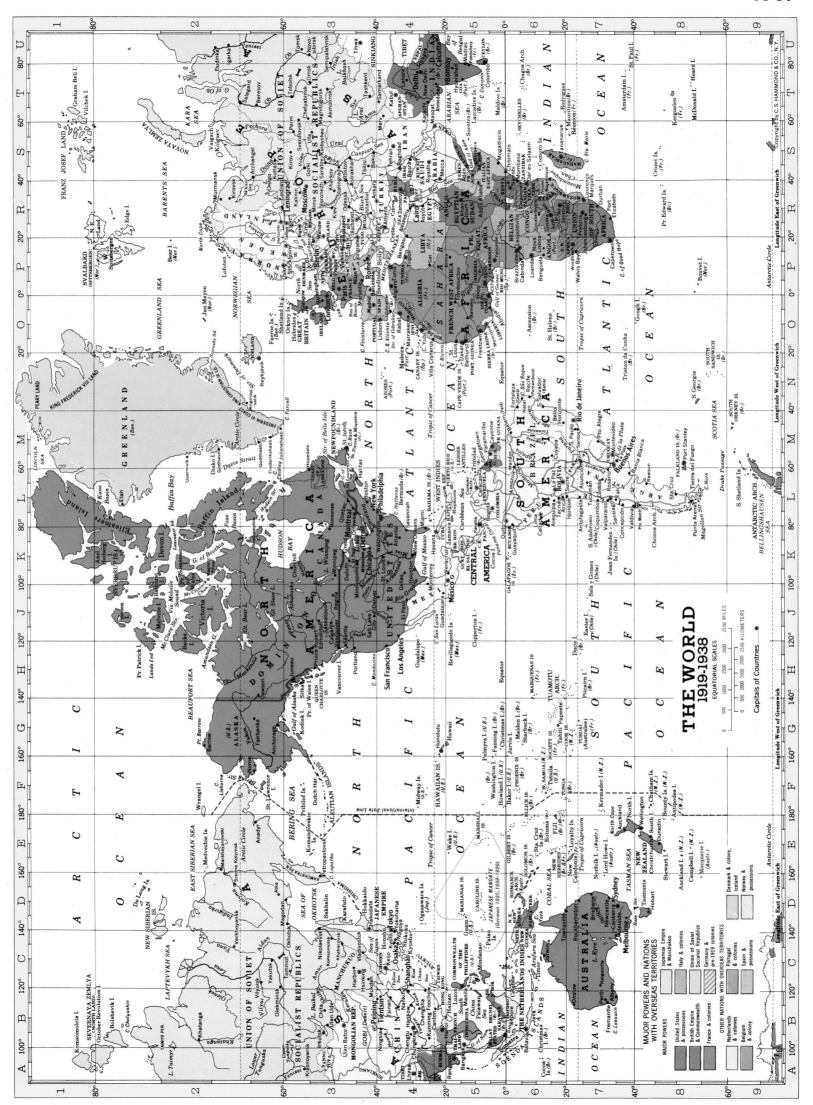

THE WORLD
1919-1938

EQUATORIAL SCALES

Capitals of Countries........⊛

MAJOR POWERS AND NATIONS WITH OVERSEAS TERRITORIES

MAJOR POWERS

- United States & possessions
- British Empire & Commonwealth
- France & colonies

OTHER NATIONS WITH OVERSEAS TERRITORIES

- Netherlands & colonies
- Belgium & colony
- Portugal & colonies
- Spain & possessions
- Denmark & possessions, Iceland
- Norway & possessions

Japanese Empire & Manchukuo
Italy & colonies
Union of Soviet Socialist Republics
Germany & pre-1919 colonies

Copyright by C. S. HAMMOND & CO., N.Y.

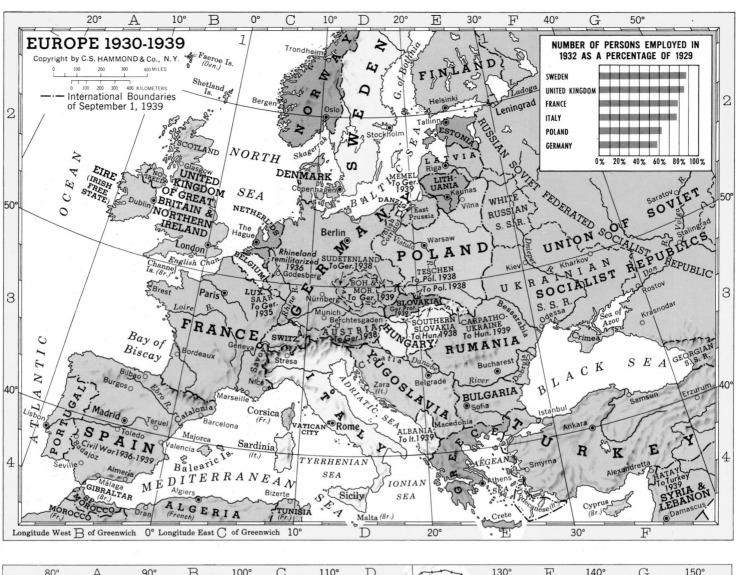

EUROPE 1930-1939

Copyright by C.S. Hammond & Co., N.Y.

— — — International Boundaries
of September 1, 1939

NUMBER OF PERSONS EMPLOYED IN 1932 AS A PERCENTAGE OF 1929

SWEDEN
UNITED KINGDOM
FRANCE
ITALY
POLAND
GERMANY

0% 20% 40% 60% 80% 100%

Longitude West B of Greenwich   0° Longitude East C of Greenwich   10°   D   20°   E   30°   F

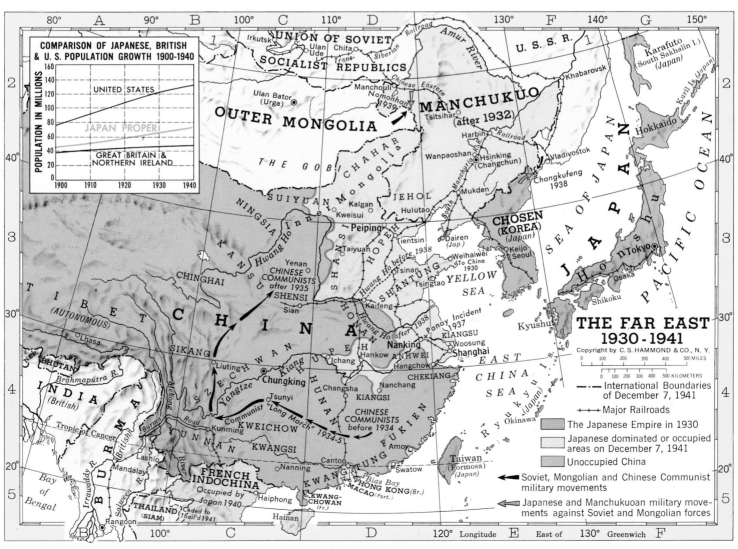

COMPARISON OF JAPANESE, BRITISH & U.S. POPULATION GROWTH 1900-1940

UNITED STATES

JAPAN PROPER

GREAT BRITAIN & NORTHERN IRELAND

1900 1910 1920 1930 1940

POPULATION IN MILLIONS

THE FAR EAST 1930-1941

Copyright by C.S. HAMMOND & CO., N.Y.

0 100 200 300 400 500 MILES

0 100 200 300 400 500 KILOMETERS

—·—·— International Boundaries
of December 7, 1941

+—+—+ Major Railroads

The Japanese Empire in 1930

Japanese dominated or occupied
areas on December 7, 1941

Unoccupied China

➤ Soviet, Mongolian and Chinese Communist
military movements

➤ Japanese and Manchukuoan military movements against Soviet and Mongolian forces

100°   C   120° Longitude   E   East of   130° Greenwich   F

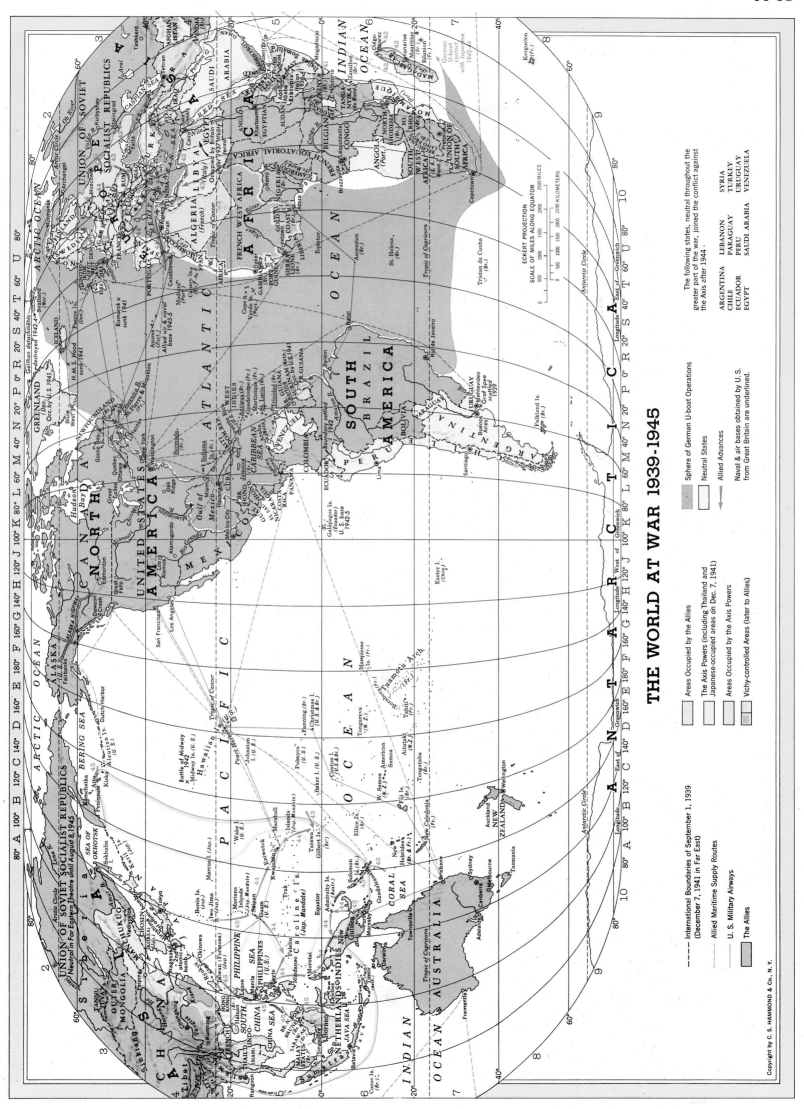

THE WORLD AT WAR 1939-1945

ECKERT PROJECTION
SCALE OF MILES ALONG EQUATOR

The following states, neutral throughout the greater part of the war, joined the conflict against the Axis after 1944.

ARGENTINA	LEBANON	SYRIA
CHILE	PARAGUAY	TURKEY
ECUADOR	PERU	URUGUAY
EGYPT	SAUDI ARABIA	VENEZUELA

— — — International Boundaries of September 1, 1939 (December 7, 1941 in Far East)

———— Allied Maritime Supply Routes

- - - - U. S. Military Airways

The Allies

Sphere of German U-boat Operations

Neutral States

Allied Advances

Naval & air bases obtained by U.S. from Great Britain are underlined.

Areas Occupied by the Allies

The Axis Powers (including Thailand and Japanese-occupied areas on Dec. 7, 1941)

Areas Occupied by the Axis Powers

Vichy-controlled Areas (later to Allies)

Copyright by C. S. HAMMOND & Co., N. Y.

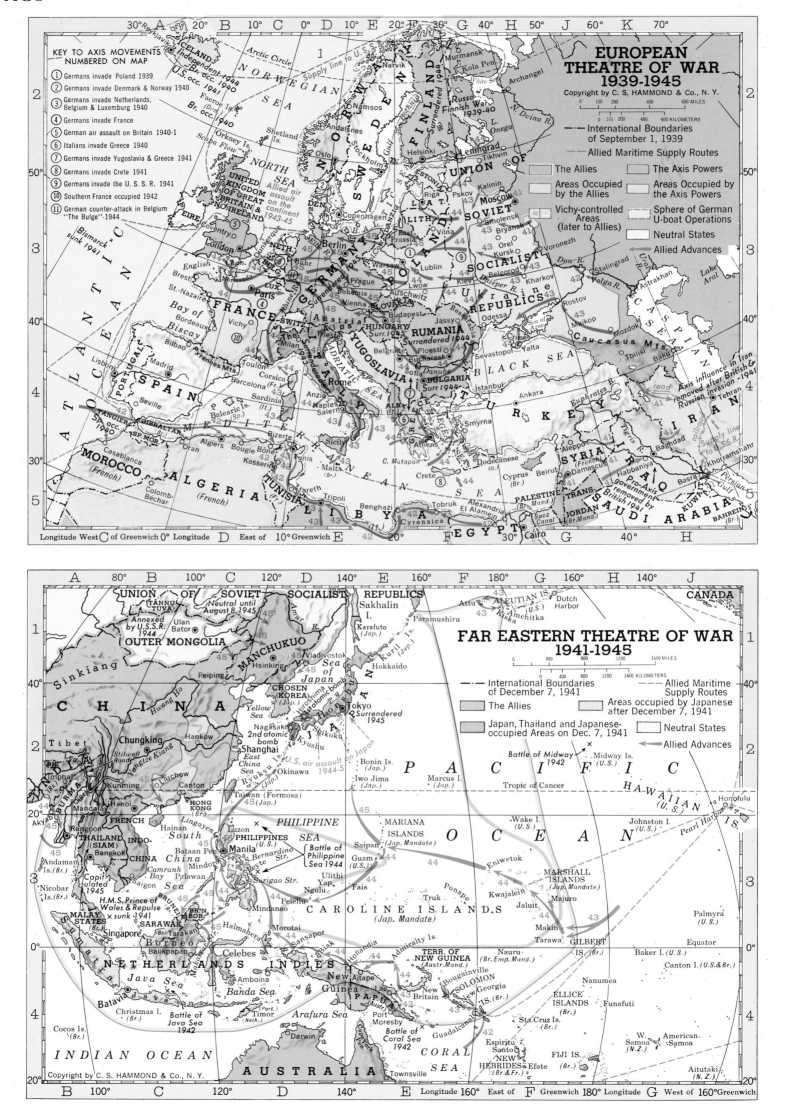

EUROPEAN THEATRE OF WAR 1939-1945

Copyright by C. S. HAMMOND & Co., N. Y.

KEY TO AXIS MOVEMENTS NUMBERED ON MAP

1. Germans invade Poland 1939
2. Germans invade Denmark & Norway 1940
3. Germans invade Netherlands, Belgium & Luxemburg 1940
4. Germans invade France
5. German air assault on Britain 1940-1
6. Italians invade Greece 1940
7. Germans invade Yugoslavia & Greece 1941
8. Germans invade Crete 1941
9. Germans invade the U.S.S.R. 1941
10. Southern France occupied 1942
11. German counter-attack in Belgium "The Bulge" 1944

International Boundaries of September 1, 1939
Allied Maritime Supply Routes
The Allies
The Axis Powers
Areas Occupied by the Allies
Areas Occupied by the Axis Powers
Vichy-controlled Areas (later to Allies)
Sphere of German U-boat Operations
Neutral States
Allied Advances

FAR EASTERN THEATRE OF WAR 1941-1945

International Boundaries of December 7, 1941
Allied Maritime Supply Routes
The Allies
Areas occupied by Japanese after December 7, 1941
Japan, Thailand and Japanese-occupied Areas on Dec. 7, 1941
Neutral States
Allied Advances

Copyright by C. S. HAMMOND & Co., N. Y.

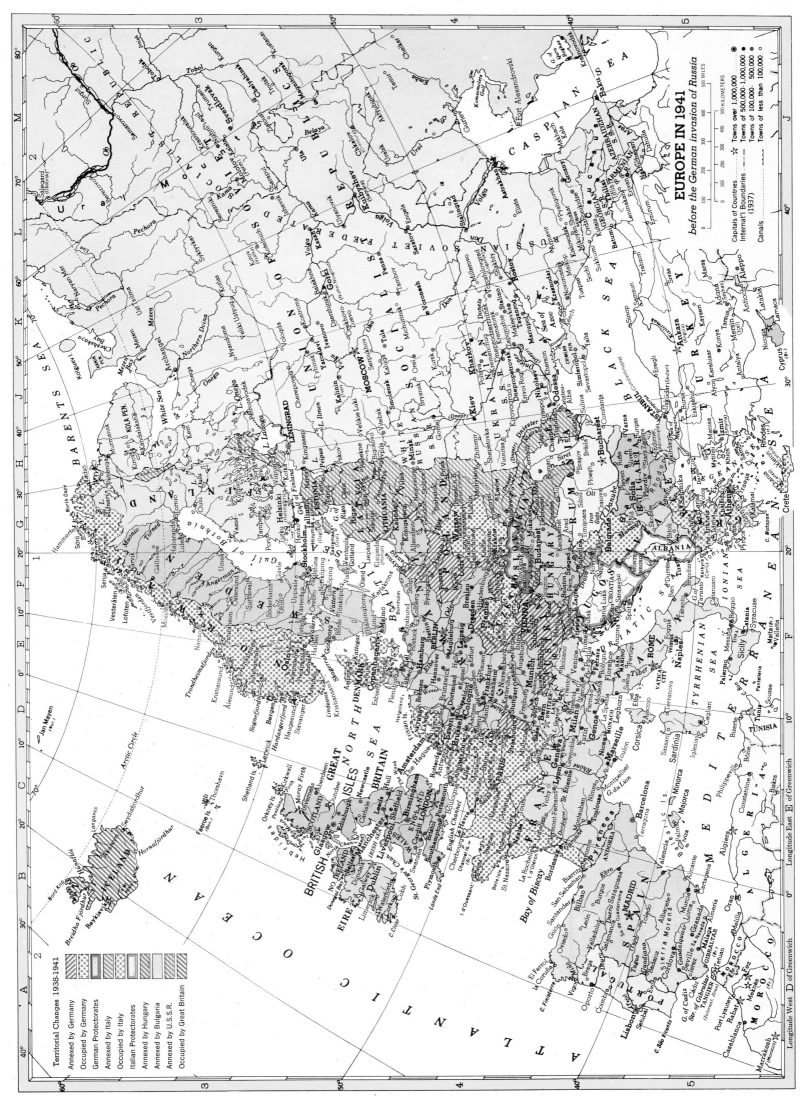

EUROPE IN 1941
before the German invasion of Russia

Capitals of Countries .... ⊛
Internat'l Boundaries ....
(1937)
Canals ....

Towns over 1,000,000 .... ★
Towns 500,000-1,000,000 ..... ●
Towns 100,000-500,000 ...... ■
Towns of less than 100,000 .. ○

500 MILES
100 200 300 400 500 KILOMETERS

Territorial Changes 1938-1941

Annexed by Germany
Occupied by Germany
German Protectorates
Annexed by Italy
Occupied by Italy
Italian Protectorates
Annexed by Hungary
Annexed by Bulgaria
Annexed by U.S.S.R.
Occupied by Great Britain

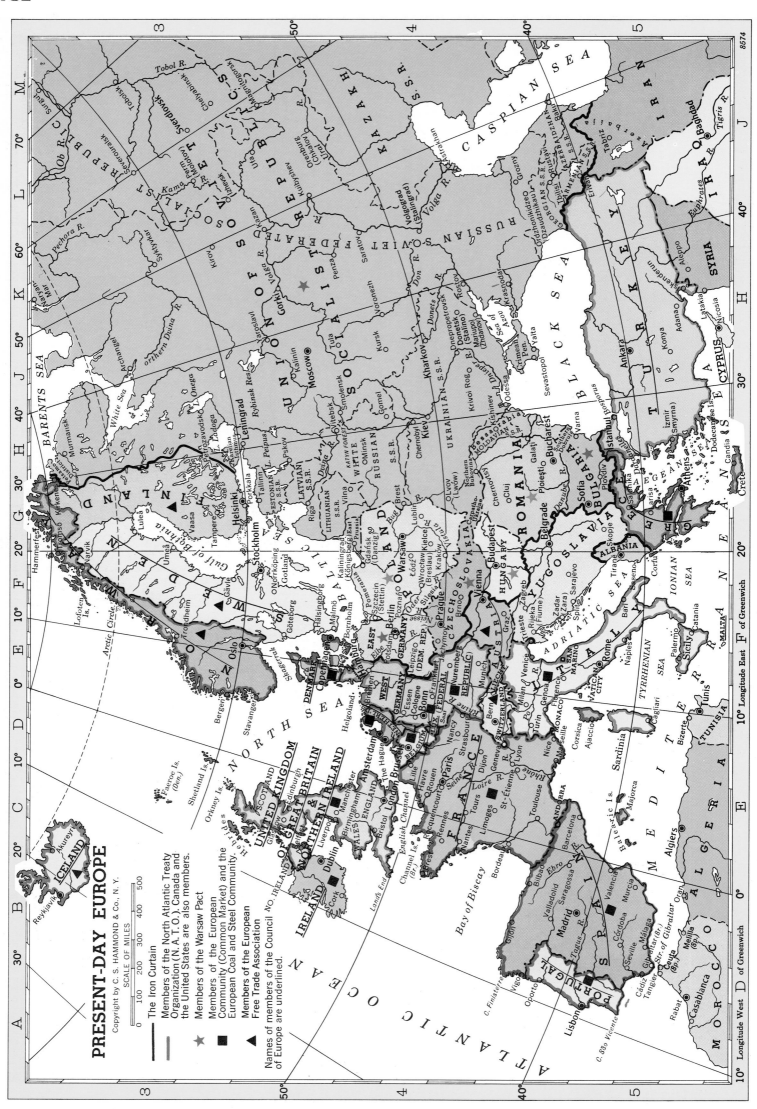

PRESENT-DAY EUROPE

Copyright by C. S. HAMMOND & Co., N.Y.

SCALE OF MILES

0 100 200 300 400 500

	The Iron Curtain
	Members of the North Atlantic Treaty Organization (N.A.T.O.) Canada and the United States are also members.
★	Members of the Warsaw Pact
■	Members of the European Community (Common Market) and the European Coal and Steel Community.
▲	Members of the European Free Trade Association

Names of members of the Council of Europe are underlined.

EUROPE
PHYSICAL

Copyright by C.S. HAMMOND & CO., N.Y.

Mountain Altitudes in Feet

THE MIDDLE EAST SINCE 1945

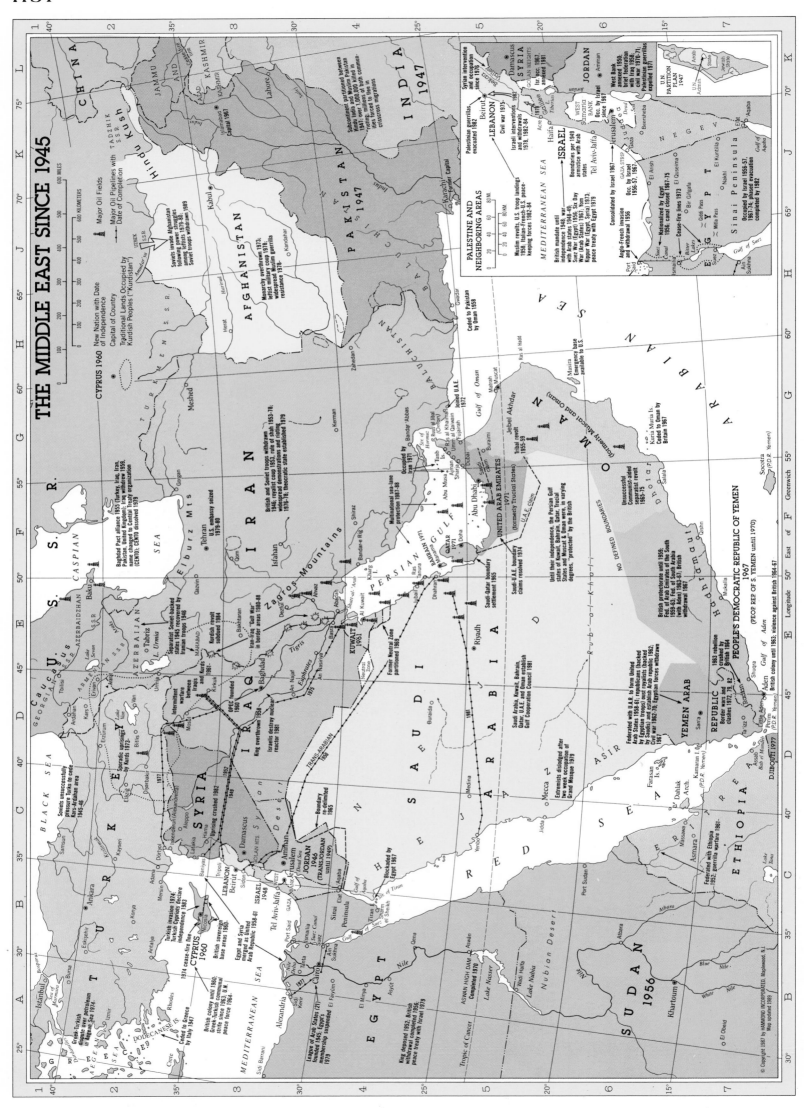

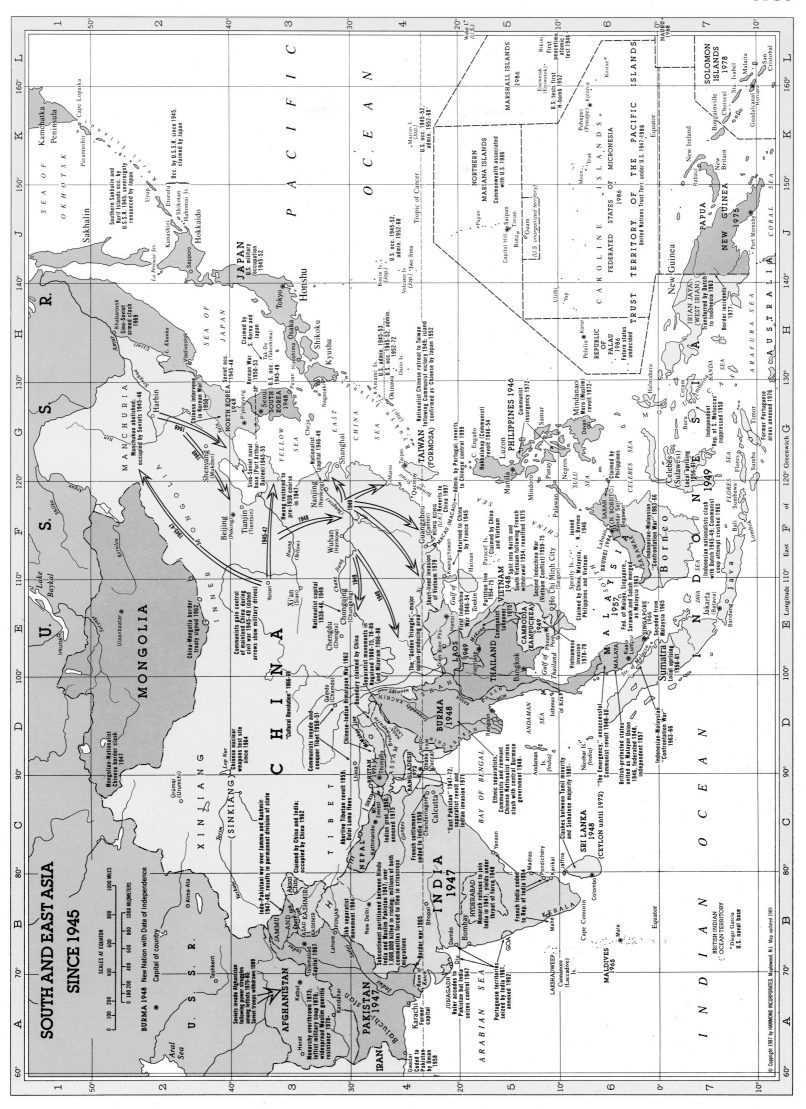

SOUTH AND EAST ASIA SINCE 1945

SCALES AT EQUATOR

BURMA 1948 New Nation with Date of Independence

● Capital of country

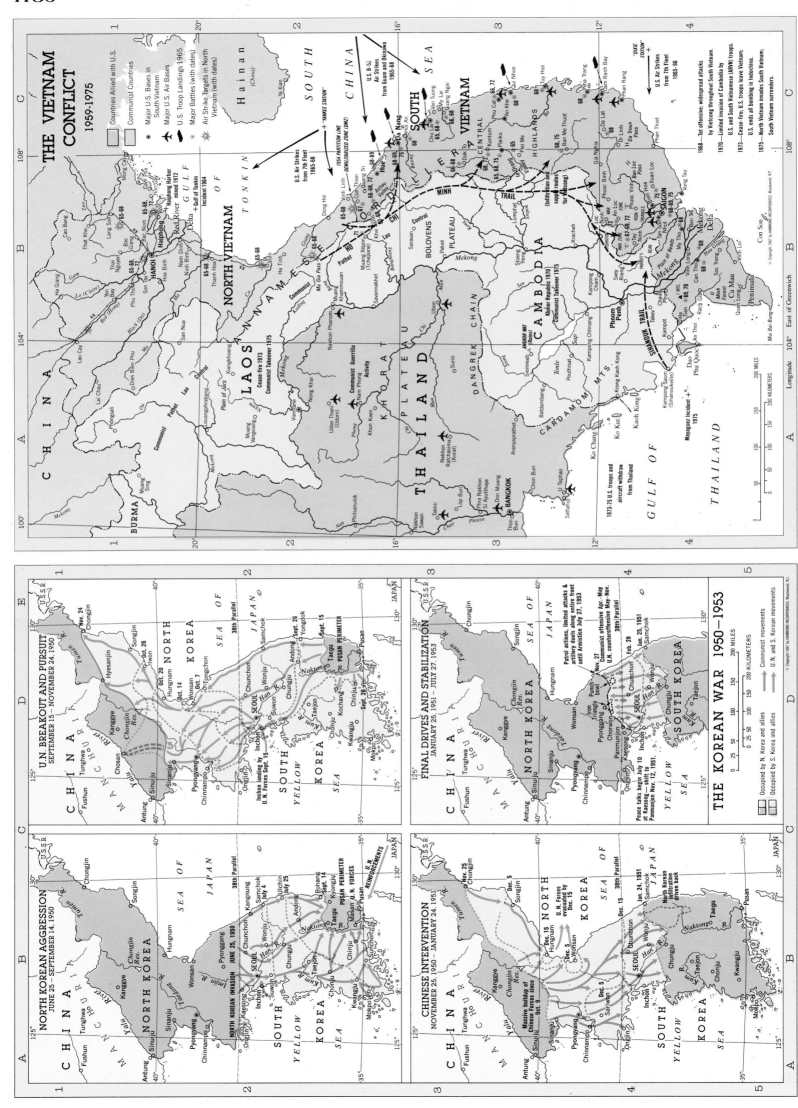

THE VIETNAM CONFLICT
1959-1975

Countries Allied with U.S.
Communist Countries
● Major U.S. Bases in South Vietnam
✈ Major U.S. Air Bases
◆ U.S. Troop Landings 1965
※ Major Battles (with dates)
✳ Air Strike Targets in North Vietnam (with dates)

1968—Tet offensive, widespread attacks by Vietcong throughout South Vietnam.
1970—Limited invasion of Cambodia by U.S. and South Vietnamese (ARVN) troops.
1973—Cease-fire; U.S. troops leave Vietnam. U.S. ends all bombing in Indochina.
1975—North Vietnam invades South Vietnam; South Vietnam surrenders.

1973-75 U.S. troops and aircraft withdraw from Thailand

Mayaguez Incident 1975

THE KOREAN WAR 1950-1953

NORTH KOREAN AGGRESSION
JUNE 25—SEPTEMBER 14, 1950

U.N. BREAKOUT AND PURSUIT
SEPTEMBER 15—NOVEMBER 24, 1950

CHINESE INTERVENTION
NOVEMBER 25, 1950—JANUARY 24, 1951

FINAL DRIVES AND STABILIZATION
JANUARY 25, 1951—JULY 27, 1953

Occupied by N. Korea and allies
Occupied by U.N. and allies

Communist movements
U.N. and S. Korean movements

Occupied by N. Korea and allies
Occupied by U.N. and allies

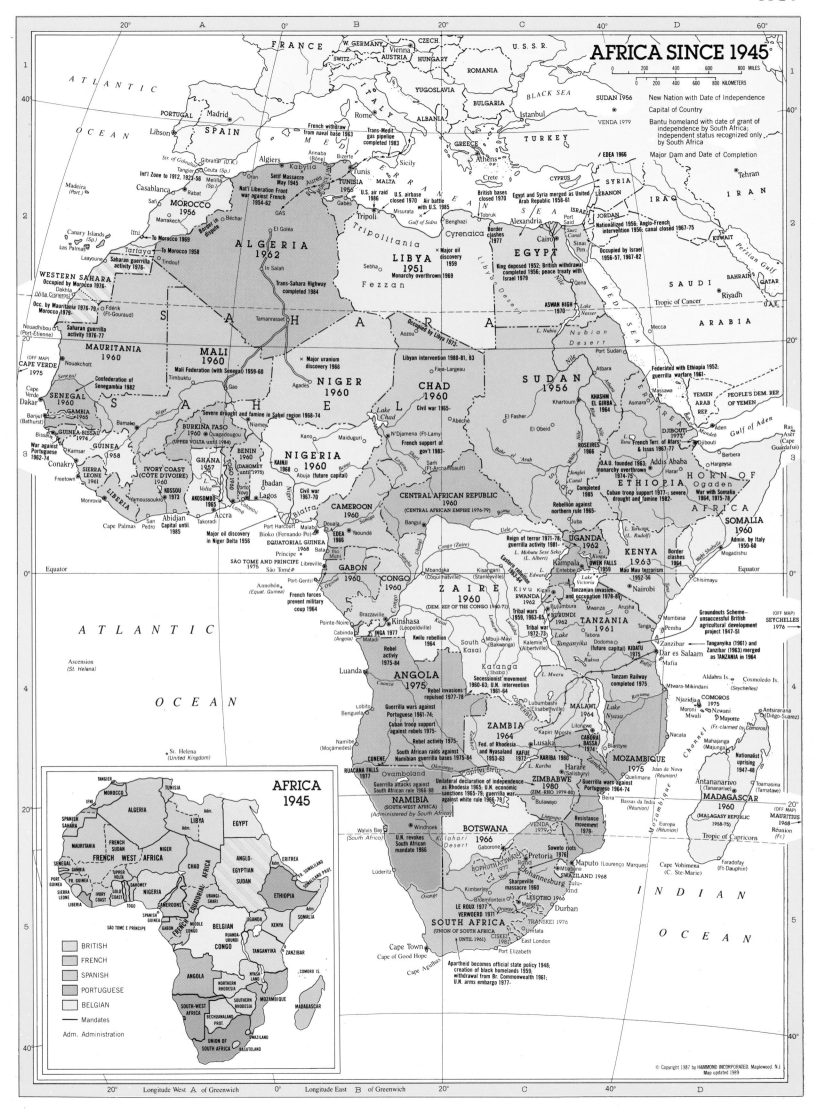

AFRICA SINCE 1945

SUDAN 1956   New Nation with Date of Independence

●   Capital of Country

VENDA 1979   Bantu homeland with date of grant of independence by South Africa; Independent status recognized only by South Africa

EDEA 1966   Major Dam and Date of Completion

AFRICA 1945

BRITISH
FRENCH
SPANISH
PORTUGUESE
BELGIAN
Mandates
Adm. Administration

© Copyright 1987 by HAMMOND INCORPORATED, Maplewood, N.J.
Map updated 1989

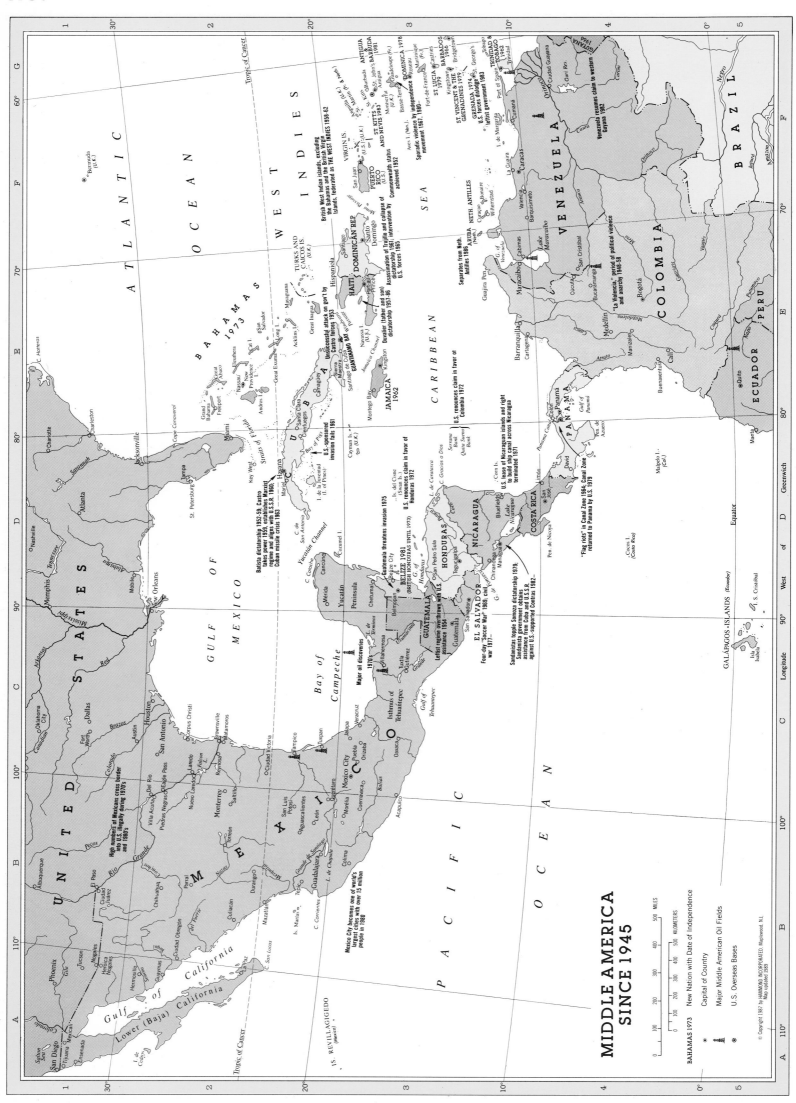

MIDDLE AMERICA
SINCE 1945

BAHAMAS 1973   New Nation with Date of Independence

⊛   Capital of Country

⬥   Major Middle American Oil Fields

⊛   U.S. Overseas Bases

© Copyright 1987 by HAMMOND INCORPORATED, Maplewood, N.J.
May updated 1989

MILES
0   100   200   300   400   500

KILOMETERS
0   100 200   300   400   500

British West Indian Islands, excluding
the Bahamas and the British Virgin
Islands, federated as THE WEST INDIES 1958-62

Commonwealth status
achieved 1952

Sporadic violence from Neth.
movement 1967. 1980-

Separates from Neth.
Antilles 1986

U.S. renounces claim in favor of
Colombia 1972

U.S. renounces claim in favor of
Honduras 1972

U.S. lease of Nicaraguan islands and right
to build ship canal across Nicaragua
terminated 1971

"Flag riots" in Canal Zone 1964. Canal
Zone returned to Panama by U.S. 1979

Sandinista government obtains
assistance from Cuba and U.S.S.R.
against U.S.-supported Contras 1982-

Sandinistas topple Somoza dictatorship 1979.

Four-day "Soccer War" 1969. civil
war 1977-

Leftist regime overthrown with U.S.
assistance 1954

BELIZE 1981
(BRITISH HONDURAS UNTIL 1973)

Guatemala threatens invasion 1975

Major oil discoveries
1970's

Mexico City becomes one of world's
largest cities with over 15 million
people in 1980

High numbers of Mexicans cross border
into U.S. illegally during 1970's
and 1980's

Batista dictatorship 1952-59. Castro
takes power 1959, establishes Marxist
regime and aligns with U.S.S.R. 1960.
Cuban missile crisis 1963

Unsuccessful attack on gov't by
Castro forces 1953

GUANTANAMO BAY
(U.S.)

U.S.-sponsored
invasion fails 1961

Duvalier (father and son)
dictatorship 1957-86

Assassination of Trujillo and collapse of
dictatorship 1961: intervention by
U.S. forces 1965

Venezuela resumes claim to western
Guyana 1982

"La Violencia," period of political violence
and anarchy 1946-58

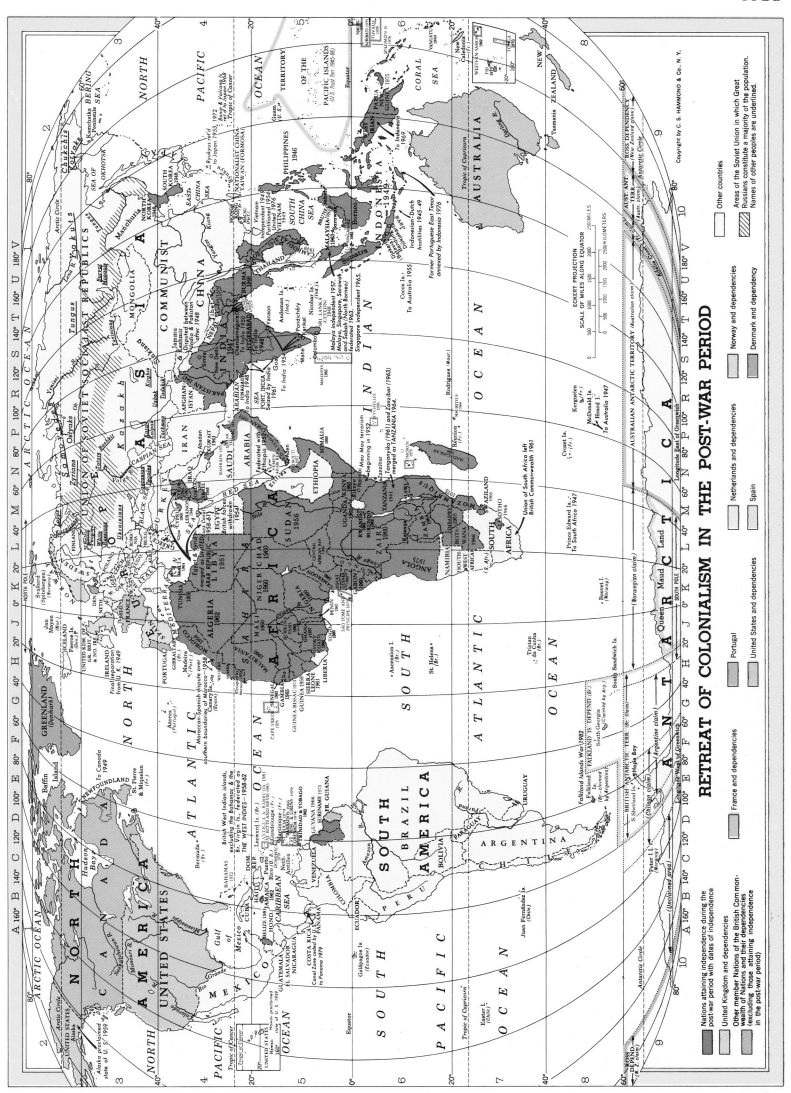

RETREAT OF COLONIALISM IN THE POST-WAR PERIOD

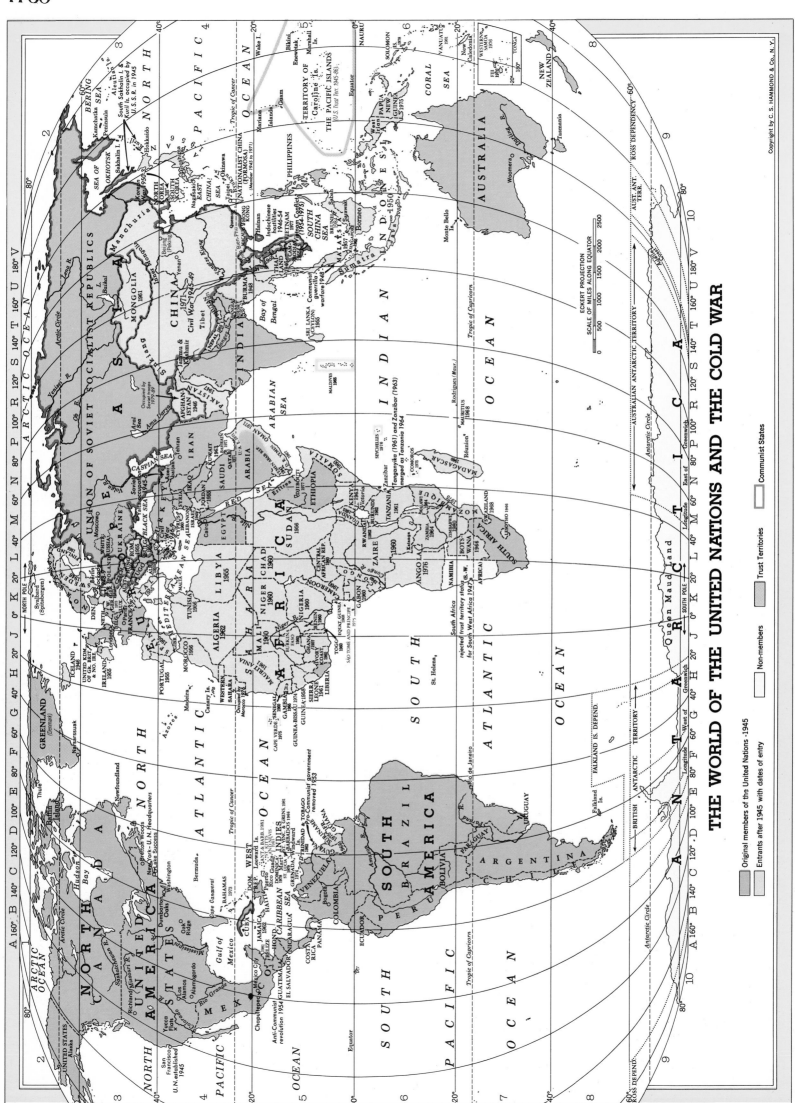

THE WORLD OF THE UNITED NATIONS AND THE COLD WAR

Original members of the United Nations -1945

Entrants after 1945 with dates of entry

Non-members

Trust Territories

Communist States

ECKERT PROJECTION
SCALE OF MILES ALONG EQUATOR
0   500   1000   1500   2000   2500

Copyright by C. S. HAMMOND & Co., N. Y.

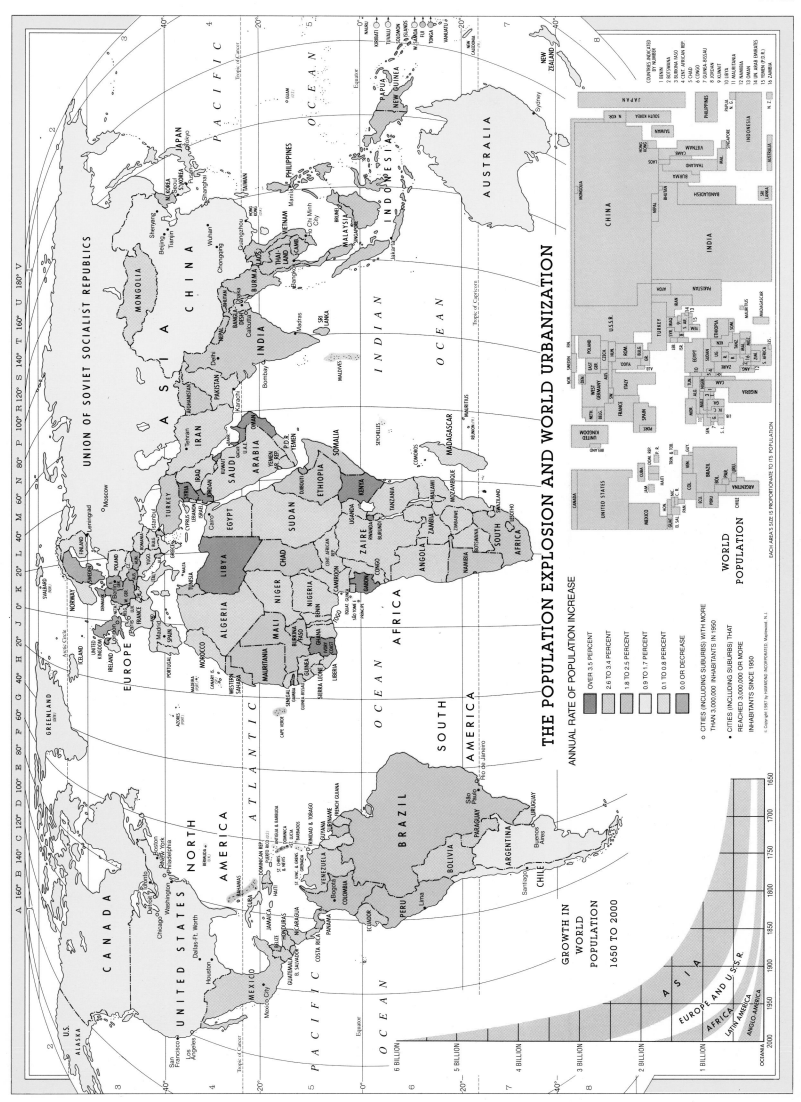

THE POPULATION EXPLOSION AND WORLD URBANIZATION

ANNUAL RATE OF POPULATION INCREASE

- OVER 3.5 PERCENT
- 2.6 TO 3.4 PERCENT
- 1.8 TO 2.5 PERCENT
- 0.9 TO 1.7 PERCENT
- 0.1 TO 0.8 PERCENT
- 0.0 OR DECREASE

○ CITIES (INCLUDING SUBURBS) WITH MORE THAN 3,000,000 INHABITANTS IN 1950

● CITIES (INCLUDING SUBURBS) THAT REACHED 3,000,000 OR MORE INHABITANTS SINCE 1950

ⓒ Copyright 1987 by HAMMOND INCORPORATED, Maplewood, N.J.

WORLD POPULATION

EACH AREA'S SIZE IS PROPORTIONATE TO ITS POPULATION

COUNTRIES INDICATED BY NUMBER
1 BENIN
2 BOTSWANA
3 BURKINA FASO
4 CENT. AFRICAN REP.
5 CHAD
6 CONGO
7 GUINEA-BISSAU
8 JORDAN
9 KUWAIT
10 LIBYA
11 MAURITANIA
12 NAMIBIA
13 OMAN
14 UN. ARAB EMIRATES
15 YEMEN (P.D.R.)
16 ZAMBIA

GROWTH IN WORLD POPULATION 1650 TO 2000

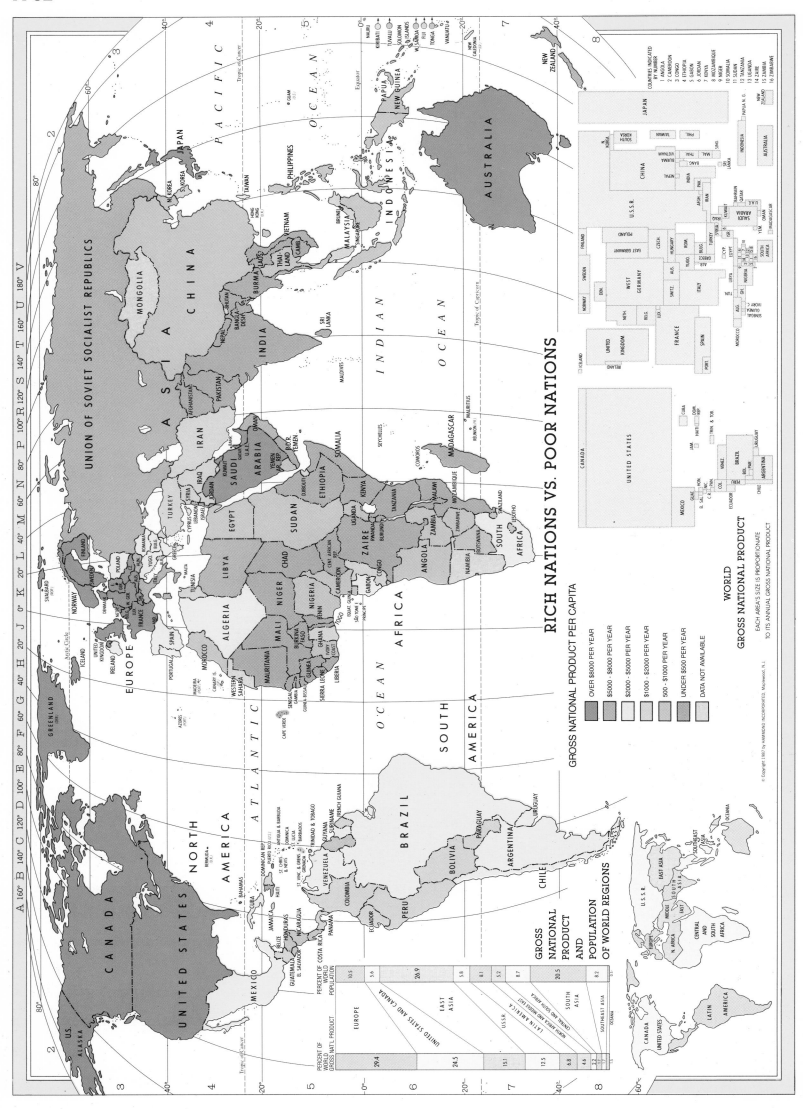

RICH NATIONS VS. POOR NATIONS

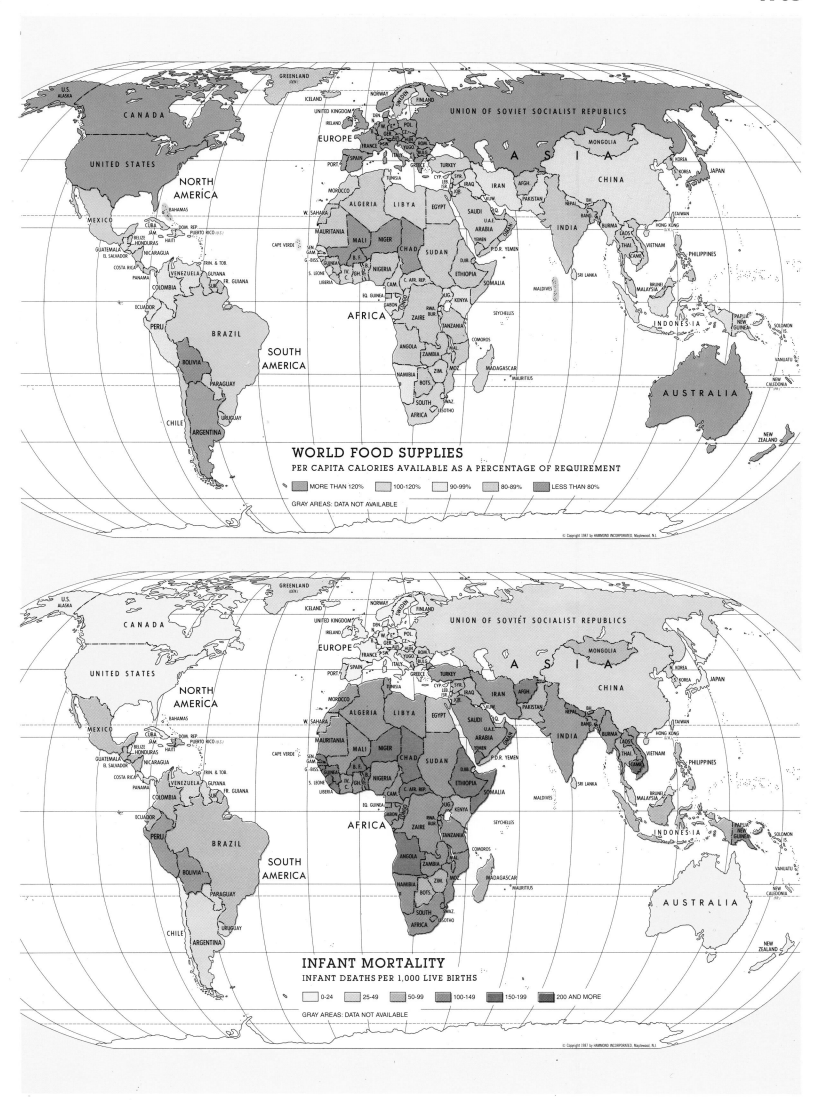

WORLD FOOD SUPPLIES
PER CAPITA CALORIES AVAILABLE AS A PERCENTAGE OF REQUIREMENT

MORE THAN 120% 100-120% 90-99% 80-89% LESS THAN 80%

GRAY AREAS: DATA NOT AVAILABLE

© Copyright 1987 by HAMMOND INCORPORATED, Maplewood, N.J.

INFANT MORTALITY
INFANT DEATHS PER 1,000 LIVE BIRTHS

0-24 25-49 50-99 100-149 150-199 200 AND MORE

GRAY AREAS: DATA NOT AVAILABLE

© Copyright 1987 by HAMMOND INCORPORATED, Maplewood, N.J.

TIME CHART

Man first learned to domesticate animals and to gather and store grains about 8000 B.C. in the hill country of the Middle East. Gradually man learned improved techniques of food-production: the sowing of seed, cultivation and irrigation. Pottery first appeared in the Near East around 5000 B.C.

The first use of copper metal occurred around 4000 B.C. in Anatolia and Iran.

DATE	AMERICAN INDIANS	BLACK AFRICANS	NORTH AFRICANS	EGYPTIANS	ARABIANS	IRANIANS	HEBREWS	PHOENICIANS	MESOPOTAMIANS	HITTITES	HELLENES (GREEKS)	AEGEANS
LATE STONE AGE												
5000 B.C.				Settled communities in the Nile Valley					Early communities in the Tigris-Euphrates Valley			
4000				Upper and Lower Kingdoms		Elamite civilization emerges			Growth of Sumerian cities			
3000				Egyptian hieroglyphics Menes unifies Egypt c. 2900		ELAM			Cuneiform writing 1st dynasty of Ur		Migration of Greek-speaking peoples	
				OLD KDM. 2615–1991 Pyramid Age				Phoenicians occupy coastal areas	Sargon I Akkadian dynasty		Aeolian & Achaean invasions	
2000 B.C.		HITTITE KDM. ASSYRIA BABYLONIAN EMP. EGYPTIAN KDM.		MIDDLE KDM. 1991–1570		Wars with Babylon	Abraham	Extensive Mediterranean trade	BABYLONIA ASSYRIA OLD BABYLONIAN EMPIRE	Early Hittite Kingdoms	Palace at Knossos	MINOAN CIVILIZATION
1750		ANCIENT EMPIRES Assyrian Empire 7th Cent. B.C.		Hyksos invaders					Hammurabi c. 1700	Labarnas est. Empire c. 1700	Height of Cretan culture	
1500	Early Pueblo culture in N. Amer			NEW KINGDOM 1570–1065 Thutmose III				Egyptian rule	Mitanni Kdm. ASSYRIA Kassite rule	HITTITE EMPIRE Iron weapons introduced	Mycenae Ionian invasion	Fall of Crete 1400
				Ikhnaton						Battle of Kadesh 1296		
1250				Rameses II			Exodus c. 1200 Conquest of Canaan		Shalman-eser I		Trojan War c. 1190	
				Invasion of Sea Peoples					Tiglath-pileser I	Hittites driven from Asia Minor	Dorian invasion	
1000 B.C.	Mayas enter Cent. Amer.		Utica founded by Phoenicians		Minaean Kdm.	Golden Age of Elam	David		Aramaean invasion			

A Graphic History of Mankind

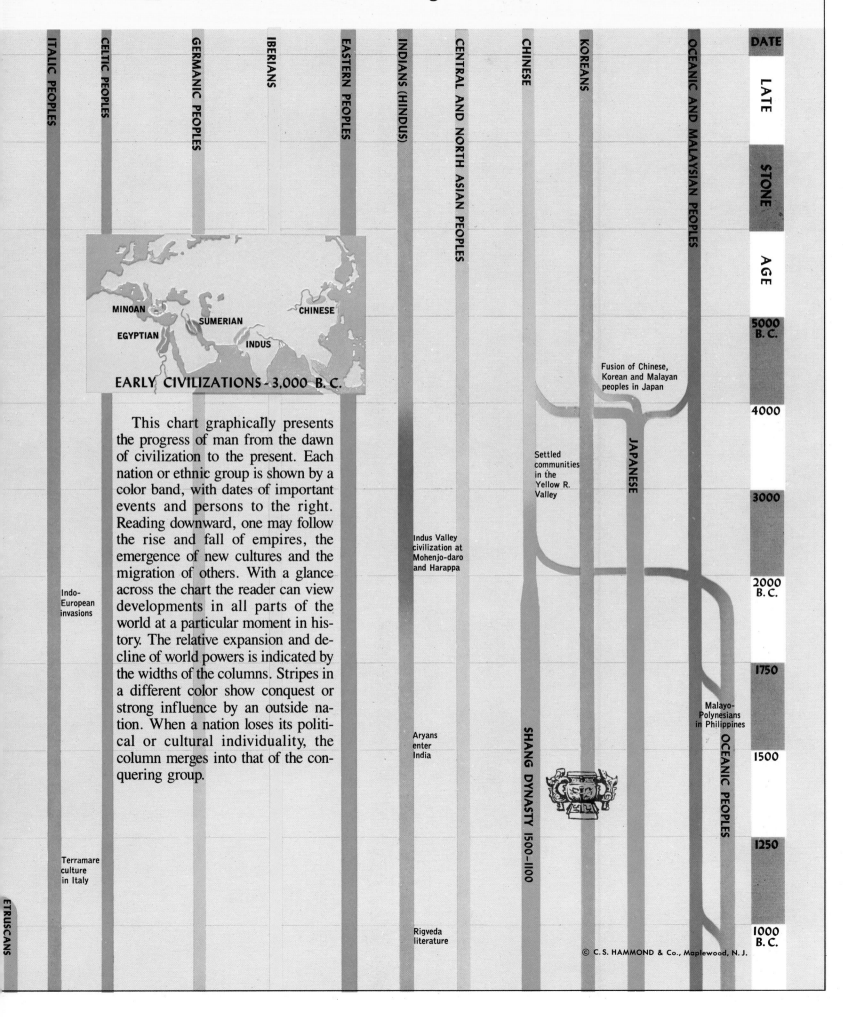

EARLY CIVILIZATIONS - 3,000 B.C.

MINOAN · EGYPTIAN · SUMERIAN · INDUS · CHINESE

This chart graphically presents the progress of man from the dawn of civilization to the present. Each nation or ethnic group is shown by a color band, with dates of important events and persons to the right. Reading downward, one may follow the rise and fall of empires, the emergence of new cultures and the migration of others. With a glance across the chart the reader can view developments in all parts of the world at a particular moment in history. The relative expansion and decline of world powers is indicated by the widths of the columns. Stripes in a different color show conquest or strong influence by an outside nation. When a nation loses its political or cultural individuality, the column merges into that of the conquering group.

Column headings:
ITALIC PEOPLES · CELTIC PEOPLES · GERMANIC PEOPLES · IBERIANS · EASTERN PEOPLES · INDIANS (HINDUS) · CENTRAL AND NORTH ASIAN PEOPLES · CHINESE · KOREANS · OCEANIC AND MALAYSIAN PEOPLES

DATE · LATE STONE AGE · 5000 B.C. · 4000 · 3000 · 2000 B.C. · 1750 · 1500 · 1250 · 1000 B.C.

Events:
- ETRUSCANS
- Indo-European invasions
- Terramare culture in Italy
- Indus Valley civilization at Mohenjo-daro and Harappa
- Aryans enter India
- Rigveda literature
- Settled communities in the Yellow R. Valley
- Fusion of Chinese, Korean and Malayan peoples in Japan
- JAPANESE
- SHANG DYNASTY 1500-1100
- Malayo-Polynesians in Philippines
- OCEANIC PEOPLES

© C.S. HAMMOND & Co., Maplewood, N.J.

TIME CHART continued

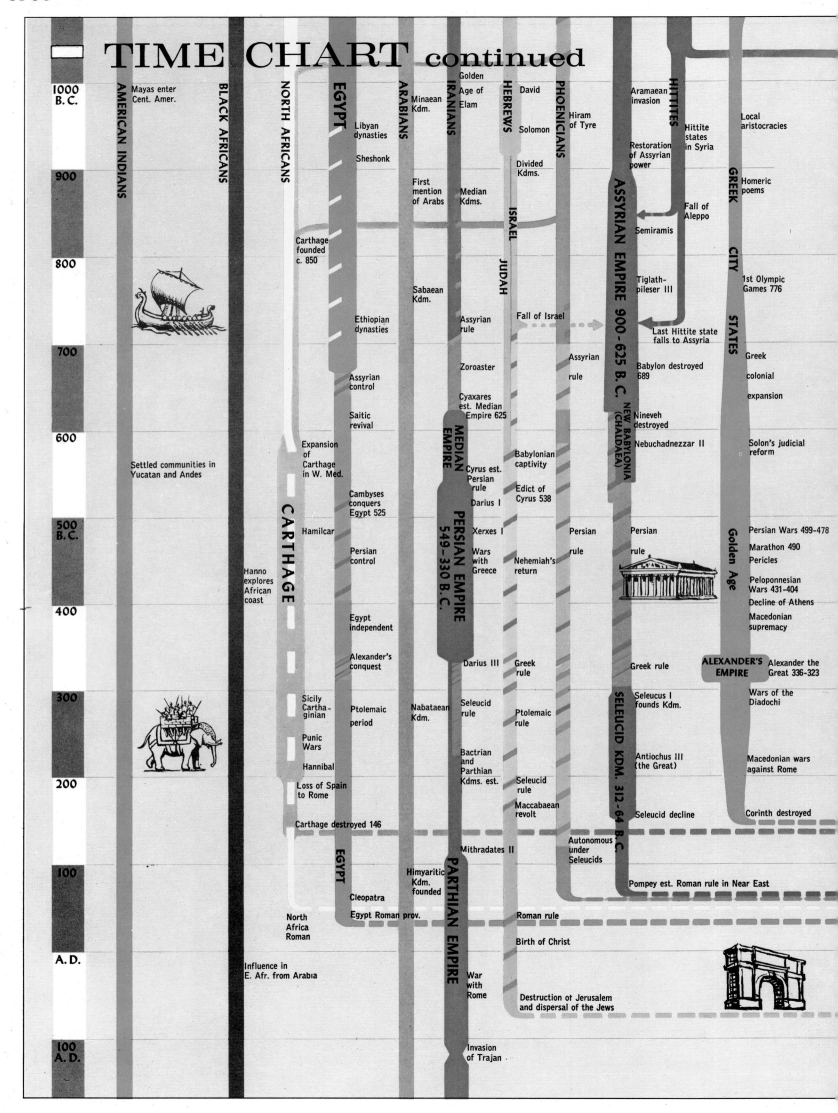

	AMERICAN INDIANS	BLACK AFRICANS	NORTH AFRICANS	EGYPT	ARABIANS	IRANIANS	HEBREWS	PHOENICIANS	HITTITES	ASSYRIAN EMPIRE	GREEK CITY STATES
1000 B.C.	Mayas enter Cent. Amer.						Golden Age of Elam / David / Solomon	Hiram of Tyre	Aramaean invasion / Hittite states in Syria	Restoration of Assyrian power	Local aristocracies
900				Libyan dynasties / Sheshonk		Minaean Kdm. / First mention of Arabs / Median Kdms.	Divided Kdms.		Fall of Aleppo	Semiramis	Homeric poems
800			Carthage founded c. 850				ISRAEL / JUDAH			Tiglath-pileser III	1st Olympic Games 776
700				Ethiopian dynasties	Sabaean Kdm.	Assyrian rule / Zoroaster	Fall of Israel	Assyrian rule	Last Hittite state falls to Assyria	Babylon destroyed 689	Greek colonial expansion
600	Settled communities in Yucatan and Andes		Expansion of Carthage in W. Med.	Assyrian control / Saitic revival		Cyaxares est. Median Empire 625 / Cyrus est. Persian rule / Darius I	Babylonian captivity / Edict of Cyrus 538	Assyrian rule		Nineveh destroyed / Nebuchadnezzar II	Solon's judicial reform
500 B.C.		Hanno explores African coast	Hamilcar	Cambyses conquers Egypt 525 / Persian control		Xerxes I / Wars with Greece	Nehemiah's return	Persian rule		Persian rule	Persian Wars 499-478 / Marathon 490 / Pericles / Peloponnesian Wars 431-404 / Decline of Athens / Golden Age
400				Egypt independent / Alexander's conquest		Darius III	Greek rule	Greek rule			Macedonian supremacy / Alexander the Great 336-323
300			Sicily Cartha-ginian / Punic Wars / Hannibal	Ptolemaic period	Nabataean Kdm.	Seleucid rule / Bactrian and Parthian Kdms. est.	Ptolemaic rule / Seleucid rule / Maccabaean revolt		Seleucus I founds Kdm. / SELEUCID KDM. 312-64 B.C.		Wars of the Diadochi / Macedonian wars against Rome
200			Loss of Spain to Rome / Carthage destroyed 146						Antiochus III (the Great) / Autonomous under Seleucids		Corinth destroyed
100		Influence in E. Afr. from Arabia	North Africa Roman	EGYPT / Cleopatra / Egypt Roman prov.	Himyaritic Kdm. founded	Mithradates II / PARTHIAN EMPIRE	Roman rule				Pompey est. Roman rule in Near East
A.D.						War with Rome	Birth of Christ / Destruction of Jerusalem and dispersal of the Jews				
100 A.D.						Invasion of Trajan					

MEDIAN EMPIRE

PERSIAN EMPIRE 549-330 B.C.

ASSYRIAN EMPIRE 900-625 B.C.

NEW BABYLONIA (CHALDAEA)

CARTHAGE

ALEXANDER'S EMPIRE

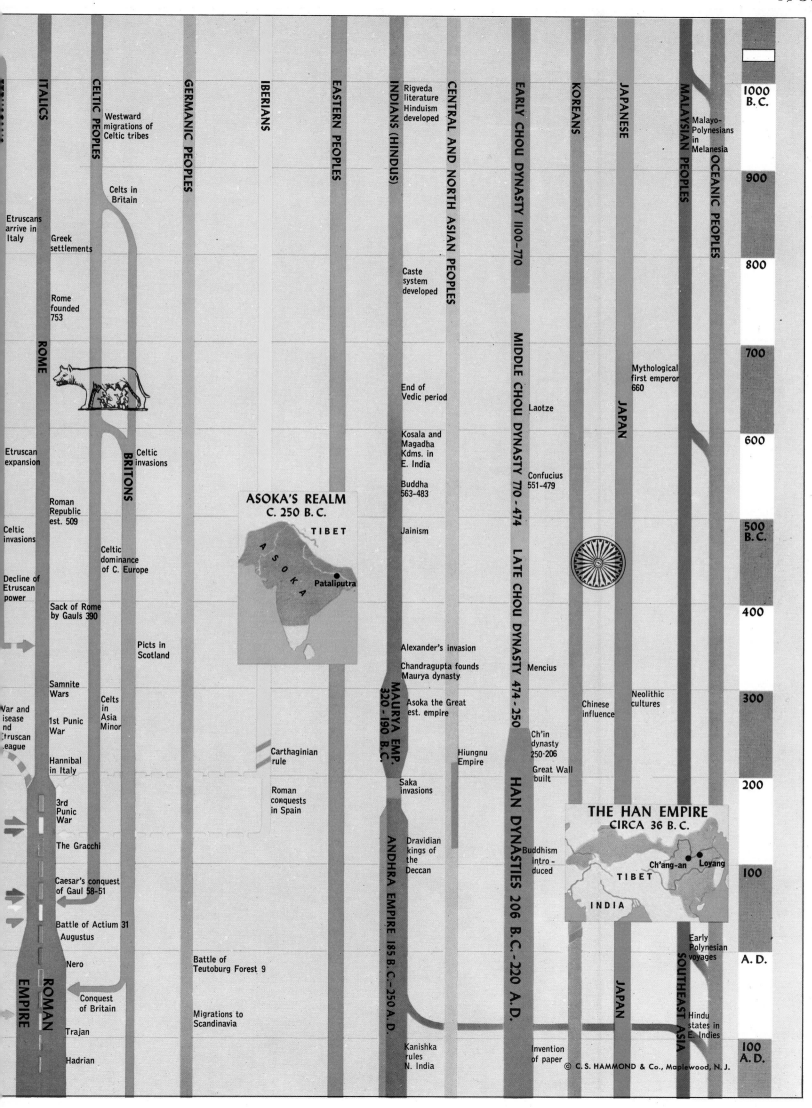

ITALICS

CELTIC PEOPLES

GERMANIC PEOPLES

IBERIANS

EASTERN PEOPLES

INDIANS (HINDUS)

CENTRAL AND NORTH ASIAN PEOPLES

EARLY CHOU DYNASTY 1100-770

KOREANS

JAPANESE

MALAYSIAN PEOPLES

OCEANIC PEOPLES

1000 B.C.

900

800

700

600

500 B.C.

400

300

200

100

A.D.

100 A.D.

Etruscans arrive in Italy

Greek settlements

Rome founded 753

ROME

Etruscan expansion

Roman Republic est. 509

Celtic invasions

Decline of Etruscan power

Sack of Rome by Gauls 390

Samnite Wars

1st Punic War

Hannibal in Italy

3rd Punic War

The Gracchi

Caesar's conquest of Gaul 58-51

Battle of Actium 31
Augustus

Nero

Conquest of Britain

Trajan

Hadrian

War and disease and Etruscan league

ROMAN EMPIRE

Westward migrations of Celtic tribes

Celts in Britain

BRITONS

Celtic invasions

Celtic dominance of C. Europe

Picts in Scotland

Celts in Asia Minor

Battle of Teutoburg Forest 9

Migrations to Scandinavia

Carthaginian rule

Roman conquests in Spain

Rigveda literature
Hinduism developed

Caste system developed

End of Vedic period

Kosala and Magadha Kdms. in E. India

Buddha 563-483

Jainism

Alexander's invasion

Chandragupta founds Maurya dynasty

MAURYA EMP. 320-190 B.C.

Asoka the Great est. empire

Saka invasions

ANDHRA EMPIRE 185 B.C.-250 A.D.

Dravidian kings of the Deccan

Kanishka rules N. India

ASOKA'S REALM C. 250 B.C.

TIBET

ASOKA

Pataliputra

MIDDLE CHOU DYNASTY 770-474

LATE CHOU DYNASTY 474-250

Laotze

Confucius 551-479

Mencius

Ch'in dynasty 250-206

Great Wall built

Hiungnu Empire

HAN DYNASTIES 206 B.C.-220 A.D.

Buddhism introduced

Invention of paper

Mythological first emperor 660

JAPAN

Chinese influence

Neolithic cultures

JAPAN

Malayo-Polynesians in Melanesia

SOUTHEAST ASIA

Early Polynesian voyages

Hindu states in E. Indies

THE HAN EMPIRE CIRCA 36 B.C.

Ch'ang-an Loyang

TIBET

INDIA

© C.S. HAMMOND & Co., Maplewood, N.J.

TIME CHART continued

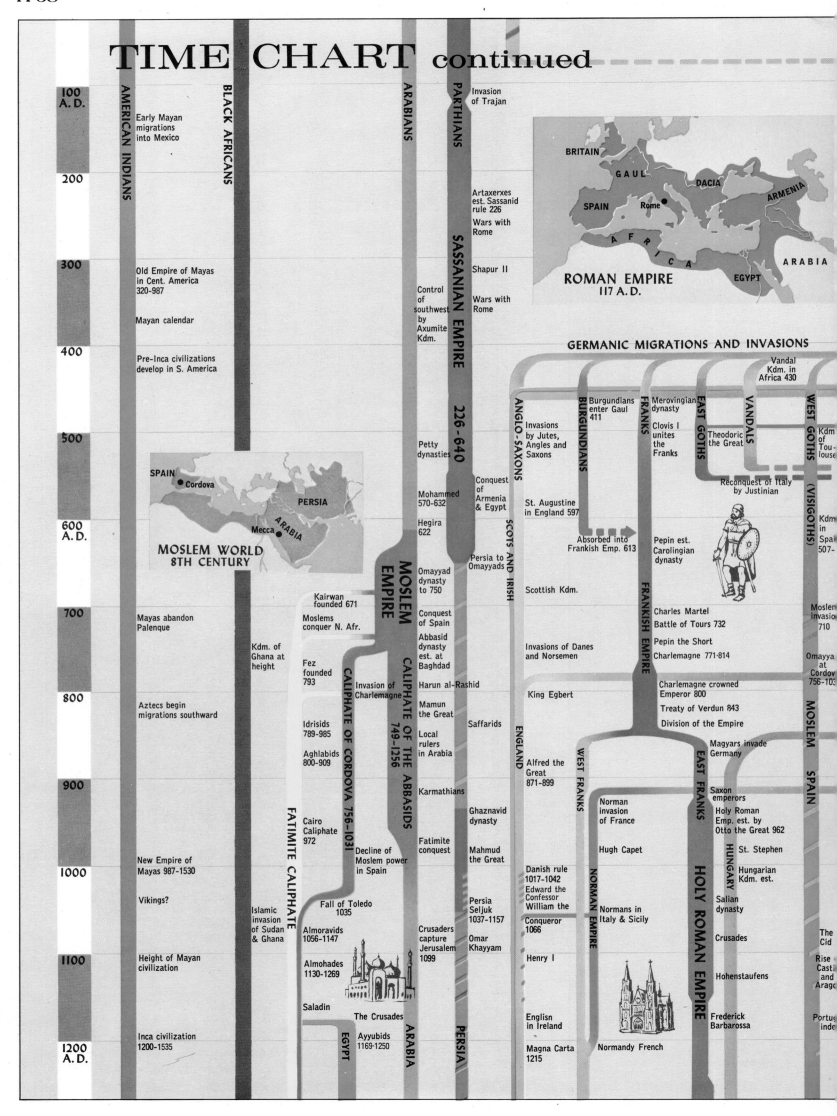

Time	AMERICAN INDIANS	BLACK AFRICANS			MOSLEM EMPIRE		CALIPHATE OF THE ABBASIDS 749-1256	ARABIANS / ARABIA	SASSANIAN EMPIRE 226-640 / PARTHIANS / PERSIA			

100 A.D. — American Indians — Black Africans — Arabians — Parthians — Invasion of Trajan — BRITAIN — GAUL — DACIA — ARMENIA — SPAIN — Rome — AFRICA — ARABIA — EGYPT

Early Mayan migrations into Mexico

ROMAN EMPIRE 117 A.D.

200 — Artaxerxes est. Sassanid rule 226 — Wars with Rome

300 — Old Empire of Mayas in Cent. America 320-987 — Mayan calendar — Control of southwest by Axumite Kdm. — Shapur II — Wars with Rome

400 — Pre-Inca civilizations develop in S. America

GERMANIC MIGRATIONS AND INVASIONS

Vandal Kdm. in Africa 430

Merovingian dynasty

500 — Petty dynasties — Conquest of Armenia & Egypt — ANGLO-SAXONS — BURGUNDIANS — Burgundians enter Gaul 411 — FRANKS — Clovis I unites the Franks — EAST GOTHS — Theodoric the Great — VANDALS — WEST GOTHS (VISIGOTHS) — Kdm of Toulouse

Invasions by Jutes, Angles and Saxons

SPAIN — Cordova — **PERSIA** — ARABIA — Mecca

MOSLEM WORLD 8TH CENTURY

Mohammed 570-632

St. Augustine in England 597

Reconquest of Italy by Justinian

Kdm in Spai 507-

600 A.D. — Hegira 622 — Persia to Omayyads — SCOTS AND IRISH — Absorbed into Frankish Emp. 613 — Pepin est. Carolingian dynasty — FRANKISH EMPIRE

Omayyad dynasty to 750 — Scottish Kdm.

700 — Mayas abandon Palenque — Kdm. of Ghana at height — Kairwan founded 671 — Moslems conquer N. Afr. — CALIPHATE OF CORDOVA 756-1031 — Conquest of Spain — Abbasid dynasty est. at Baghdad — Invasions of Danes and Norsemen — Charles Martel Battle of Tours 732 — Pepin the Short — Charlemagne 771-814 — Moslem invasio 710

Fez founded 793 — Invasion of Charlemagne — Harun al-Rashid — King Egbert — Charlemagne crowned Emperor 800 — Omayya at Cordov 756-103

800 — Aztecs begin migrations southward — Idrisids 789-985 — Mamun the Great — Saffarids — Treaty of Verdun 843 — Division of the Empire — MOSLEM SPAIN

Aghlabids 800-909 — Local rulers in Arabia — ENGLAND — WEST FRANKS — Magyars invade Germany — EAST FRANKS

900 — Alfred the Great 871-899 — Saxon emperors — HUNGARY

Cairo Caliphate 972 — Karmathians — Norman invasion of France — Holy Roman Emp. est. by Otto the Great 962 — St. Stephen

Ghaznavid dynasty — Hugh Capet — Hungarian Kdm. est.

New Empire of Mayas 987-1530 — FATIMITE CALIPHATE — Fatimite conquest — Mahmud the Great — Danish rule 1017-1042 — NORMAN EMPIRE — Salian dynasty

1000 — Vikings? — Decline of Moslem power in Spain — Edward the Confessor William the — HOLY ROMAN EMPIRE

Islamic invasion of Sudan & Ghana — Fall of Toledo 1035 — Persia Seljuk 1037-1157 — Normans in Italy & Sicily — Crusades — The Cid

Almoravids 1056-1147 — Crusaders capture Jerusalem 1099 — Omar Khayyam — William the Conqueror 1066

1100 — Height of Mayan civilization — Almohades 1130-1269 — Henry I — Hohenstaufens — Rise Casti and Arago

Saladin — English in Ireland — Frederick Barbarossa — Portu inde

Inca civilization 1200-1535 — EGYPT — The Crusades — Ayyubids 1169-1250 — ARABIA — PERSIA — Magna Carta 1215 — Normandy French

1200 A.D.

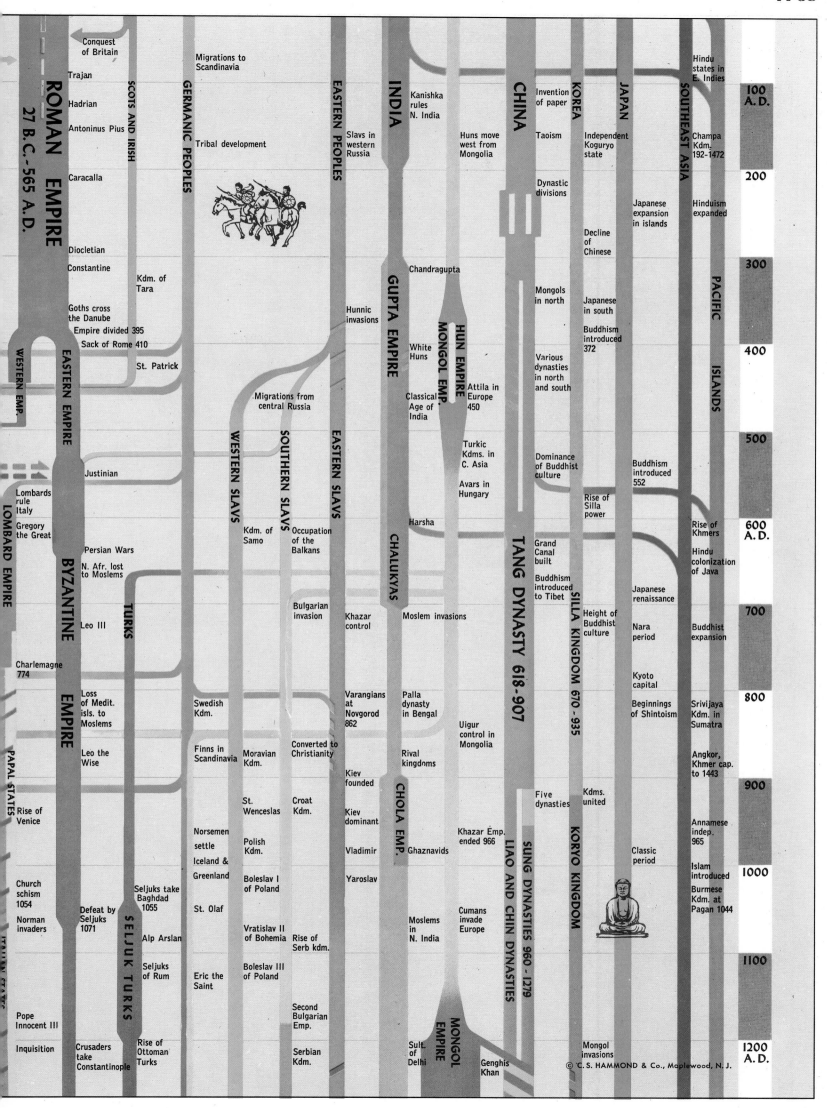

ROMAN EMPIRE 27 B.C.-565 A.D.

- Conquest of Britain
- Trajan
- Hadrian
- Antoninus Pius
- Caracalla
- Diocletian
- Constantine
- Goths cross the Danube
- Empire divided 395
- Sack of Rome 410
- St. Patrick

WESTERN EMP.

EASTERN EMPIRE

BYZANTINE EMPIRE

- Justinian
- Lombards rule Italy
- Gregory the Great
- Persian Wars
- N. Afr. lost to Moslems
- Leo III
- Charlemagne 774
- Loss of Medit. isls. to Moslems
- Leo the Wise
- Rise of Venice
- Church schism 1054
- Norman invaders
- Pope Innocent III
- Inquisition

LOMBARD EMPIRE

PAPAL STATES

SCOTS AND IRISH
- Kdm. of Tara

GERMANIC PEOPLES
- Migrations to Scandinavia
- Tribal development

TURKS
- Swedish Kdm.
- Finns in Scandinavia
- Norsemen settle Iceland & Greenland
- St. Olaf

SELJUK TURKS
- Seljuks take Baghdad 1055
- Defeat by Seljuks 1071
- Alp Arslan
- Seljuks of Rum
- Eric the Saint
- Rise of Ottoman Turks
- Crusaders take Constantinople

WESTERN SLAVS
- Migrations from central Russia
- Kdm. of Samo
- Moravian Kdm.
- St. Wenceslas
- Polish Kdm.
- Boleslav I of Poland
- Vratislav II of Bohemia
- Boleslav III of Poland

SOUTHERN SLAVS
- Occupation of the Balkans
- Bulgarian invasion
- Converted to Christianity
- Croat Kdm.
- Rise of Serb kdm.
- Second Bulgarian Emp.
- Serbian Kdm.

EASTERN PEOPLES

EASTERN SLAVS
- Slavs in western Russia
- Hunnic invasions
- Khazar control
- Varangians at Novgorod 862
- Kiev founded
- Kiev dominant
- Vladimir
- Yaroslav

INDIA
- Kanishka rules N. India
- Chandragupta

GUPTA EMPIRE
- White Huns
- Classical Age of India

CHALUKYAS
- Harsha
- Moslem invasions

CHOLA EMP.
- Palla dynasty in Bengal
- Rival kingdoms
- Ghaznavids
- Moslems in N. India
- Sult. of Delhi

HUN EMPIRE MONGOL EMP.
- Huns move west from Mongolia
- Attila in Europe 450
- Turkic Kdms. in C. Asia
- Avars in Hungary

MONGOL EMPIRE
- Khazar Emp. ended 966
- Cumans invade Europe
- Genghis Khan

CHINA
- Invention of paper
- Taoism
- Dynastic divisions
- Decline of Chinese
- Mongols in north
- Various dynasties in north and south
- Dominance of Buddhist culture
- Grand Canal built
- Buddhism introduced to Tibet
- Uigur control in Mongolia
- Five dynasties

TANG DYNASTY 618-907

LIAO AND CHIN DYNASTIES

SUNG DYNASTIES 960-1279
- Mongol invasions

KOREA
- Independent Koguryo state
- Rise of Silla power
- Kdms. united

SILLA KINGDOM 670-935

KORYO KINGDOM

JAPAN
- Japanese expansion in islands
- Japanese in south
- Buddhism introduced 372
- Buddhism introduced 552
- Japanese renaissance
- Nara period
- Kyoto capital
- Beginnings of Shintoism
- Classic period

SOUTHEAST ASIA
- Hindu states in E. Indies

PACIFIC ISLANDS
- Champa Kdm. 192-1472
- Hinduism expanded
- Rise of Khmers
- Hindu colonization of Java
- Buddhist expansion
- Srivijaya Kdm. in Sumatra
- Angkor, Khmer cap. to 1443
- Annamese indep. 965
- Islam introduced
- Burmese Kdm. at Pagan 1044

100 A.D.	
200	
300	
400	
500	
600 A.D.	
700	
800	
900	
1000	
1100	
1200 A.D.	

© C. S. HAMMOND & Co., Maplewood, N. J.

TIME CHART continued

1200 A.D.	AMERICAN INDIANS	BLACK AFRICANS	Mali & Bornu Kdms.	Hafsids 1228-1534	EGYPT — Mameluke rule 1250-1517	ARABIA	PERSIA — Conquest by Mongol Il-Khans 1256-1336	ENGLAND — Magna Carta 1215 / Edward the Confessor	Normandy French	FRANCE	HOLY ROMAN EMPIRE — Frederick Barbarossa / HUNGARY — Mongol invasion / CHRISTIAN SPAIN — Portug. indep.
1300		Baguirmi Kdm.	NORTH AFRICAN STATES		Moslem restoration		Hundred Years War with France 1339-1453	Popes at Avignon 1305-1378		GERMAN STATES	Hanseatic League
1400	Aztecs found Mexico City c. 1325 / Destruction of Mayan cities in Yucatan / Height of Inca Emp. c. 1480 / Columbus 1492	Portuguese in West Africa	Portuguese & Sp. in N. Afr.	Timurids	War of the Roses / Chaucer	Joan of Arc burned 1431 / Louis XI		Frederick Hohenzollern / John Hunyadi	Union with Poland	Henry the Navigat. / Ferdinand & Isabella
1500	Cortez conquers Mexico / Pizarro conquers Peru / Portuguese in Brazil	Songhoy Kdm.	Morocco indep. to 1912	Turkish rule 1517	Portuguese in Oman	Safavid dynasty 1499-1736	Tudors / Exploration of America / Henry VIII / Elizabeth / Spanish Armada destroyed 1588	Francis I / Religious Wars	Martin Luther / First Hapsburg Emp. / Charles V / Calvin	Battle of Mohacs 1526 / Turkish siege of Vienna / Wm. of Orange / Indep. from Sp. Hapsburgs 1581	New World Empire / Charles / SPAIN AND PORTUGAL / Phil II
1600	Jamestown 1607 / Champlain / Plymouth 1620 / New Amsterdam 1626 / La Salle	Kdm. of Benin / Slave trade	Turkish rule in N. Afr.	Abbas the Great	Shakespeare / Stuarts / Cromwell / Wm. of Orange	Louis XIV	Thirty Years War 1618-1648	United Provinces 1579-1795 / Por. Kdm.
1700 A.D.	Plains of Abraham 1759 / French & Indian War	Ashanti Kdm. / European coastal colonies	First Fr. influence in N. Afr.	Decline of Turkish control	Nadir Shah / Wahhabis control hinterland / Kajar dynasty	Union of Eng. & Scot. 1707 / Hanoverians / Treaty of Paris 1763 / Beginning of Industrial Revolution	Louis XV / French Revolution 1789	Frederick of Prussia / Frederick II (the Great)	Hungary incorp. / Maria Theresa / Batavian rep.	War of Sp. Sucn.
1800	Latin American states indep. / American Revolution 1775-1783 / Louisiana Purchase / War of 1812	Liberia independent	Fr. in Algeria	Napoleon in Egypt 1798 / Mohammed Ali	Caucasus area lost to Russia	Waterloo 1815	NAPOLEON'S EMPIRE 1804-1815 / Second Republic / Germanic Confederation	Metternich chancellor / Low Countries independent	Kdm. restored 1814 / Carlist War
1850	Maximilian 1863-1867 / Confederation 1867	UNITED STATES OF AMERICA / Civil War 1861-1865 / Spanish Amer. War 1898	COLONIAL NORTH AFRICA / Diamond rush 1870 / European colonial expansion	Fr. in Tunisia	Suez Canal 1859-1869 / Brit. control 1882	GREAT BRITAIN / Crimean War 1854-1856 / Victoria 1837-1901	FRANCE / Louis Napoleon / Franco-Prussian War / Third Rep.	GERMANY / German Emp. 1871	Dual Monarchy 1867 / Franz Josef	Congo Free State to Belg. / Wilhelmina Q. of Neth. / First Rep. 1873-1874 / Sp. Amer. War
1900	Panama Canal opened 1914 / LATIN AMERICA	CANADA / U.S. enters W.W. I 1917	Italians in Libya / Ger. col's to Brit., France & Belg.	Persian Revolution / Oil developments / Revolt against Turkey	Boer War 1899-1902 / World War I 1914-1918	World War I 1914-1918 / Defeat of Germany & Austria / Rep.	Albert I K. of Belg.	
1925	Chaco War 1932-1935 / Statute of Westminster 1931	Saudi Arabia created / Kdm. established / Brit. prot. ended 1936	IRAN	World War II 1939-1945 / Churchill 1940-1945 / Colonial withdrawal	Ger. invasion & occ.	Rise of Hitler & Nazis 1933 / World War II	BENELUX / Rep. Hungary Rep. / German invasion & occ.	Second Rep. / Civil War / Franco 1936-1975 / SPAIN AND PORTUGAL
1950	Peron in Argentina / World War II Atomic Bomb U.N. founded Korean War 1950	EGYPT / Indep. N. Afr. / New African nations / South African apartheid	Algerian War / Suez Crisis 1956 / Nasser 1954-1970 / OPEC oil embargo 1973 / Qaddafi in Libya	ARABIAN STATES / State of Israel 1948 / ISRAEL / Six-day War 1967 / Yom Kippur War 1973	Mohammed Reza Pahlavi 1941-1979	Berlin crises / de Gaulle	AUSTRIA / Divided Germany	Berlin crises / Common Market / Hung. revolt 1956 / Allied occupation
1975	Sandinistas in Nicaragua / Castro in Cuba / New Constitution 1982 / Falklands War 1982	Trade deficit / Watergate / 50 states / Civil Rights movement / Moon landings	Sadat 1970-1981 / Civil war in Lebanon	Khomeini / Iran-Iraq War	Sectarian violence in Northern Ireland / Thatcher		Common Market	Constitutional monarchy 1975

Time markers (right side): 1200 A.D. | 1300 | 1400 | 1500 | 1600 | 1700 A.D. | 1800 | 1850 | 1900 | 1925 | 1950 | 1975

ITALIAN STATES / ITALY
Pope Innocent III
Inquisition
Rise of Genoa
Dante
Height of Venetian sea power
Great Schism 1378-1417
Medici
da Vinci
Andrea Doria
Michelangelo
Galileo
sion
Mazzini
War of indep.
Cavour unifies Italy 1861
Kdm. of Italy 1870
Italo-Turkish War 1911-1912
Mussolini comes to power 1922
Abyssinia attacked 1935
World War II
Rep.

BYZANTINE GREEKS
Crusaders take Constantinople 1204
Palaeologi 1261-1453
Turks take Constantinople 1453

OTTOMAN EMPIRE 1299-1923 / TURKEY
Rise of Ottoman Turks
Mohammed I
Mohammed the Conqueror
Suleiman the Magnificent
Battle of Lepanto 1571
Vienna besieged 1683
Russo-Turkish wars
Greek War of indep. 1821-1830
Otto I
Battle of Navarino 1827
George I
Modern Olympic Games 1896
Russo-Turkish War 1877
Young Turk movement
World War I
Republic
Atatürk forms rep.
Kdm. restored 1935
German invasion & occ.
Civil War 1944-1950
Military dictatorship 1967-1974
Republic 1975
Turks invade Cyprus 1974

GREECE
Balkan Wars

SCANDINAVIA
Union of Kalmar
Finland to Sweden
Gustavus Adolphus
Charles XII
Finland to Russia 1809
Norway separate
Finland indep. 1918
German occ. of Denmark & Norway

WESTERN SLAVS
Hussite Wars
Poland and Lithuania united
Livonian War
Hapsburgs in Bohemia
John Sobieski
Bohemia to Austria
Polish partitions
Polish Kdm. under Russia
First Polish Revolution
Second Polish Revolution
Pilsudski
German control of Poland & Czech.
Holocaust Soviet satellites
Soviets invade Czechoslovakia 1968
Polish Solidarity movement

SOUTHERN SLAVS
Serbian Kdm.
Turkish control of Balkans
Austrian invasion
Serb uprising
Balkans auton.
Bulgaria & Serbia indep.
Balkan Wars
Slavic states independent
German control in Balkans
Tito in Yugoslavia 1945-1980

EASTERN SLAVS / RUSSIAN EMPIRE / U.S.S.R.
End of Mongol control
Ivan the Great
Ivan the Terrible
Romanov dynasty 1613-1917
Peter the Great
Catharine the Great
Napoleon's invasion
Crimean War 1854-1856
Central Asian expansion
Russo-Japanese War 1904-1905
World War I
Russian Revolution 1917
U.S.S.R. formed 1922
Stalin 1926-1953
World War II German invasion
Cold War with West
Sputnik 1957
Soviet occupation of Afghanistan 1979-1989

INDIA / MOGUL EMPIRE
Sult. of Delhi
Timur sacks Delhi
Vasco da Gama at Calicut 1498
Sikh religion founded
Akbar the Great
East India Company 1600
Aurangzeb 1658-1707
Clive 1725-1774
Afghan wars
Sepoy Rebellion 1857
Gandhi's passive resistance 1920's-1948
Independence of India, Pakistan & Ceylon
Border clash with China 1962
Bangladesh 1971
Sikh separatism

MONGOL EMPIRE
Genghis Khan 1206-1227
Khanate of the Golden Horde
Jagatai
Tatar Empire 1368-1409
Timur (Tamerlane)
Volga Khanates lost to Russia
Manchu conquest

YÜAN DYNASTY 1260-1368 / MING DYNASTY 1368-1644 / MANCHU (CH'ING) DYNASTY 1644-1912
Kublai Khan
Marco Polo in China
Growth of Moslems
Christian missionaries
Portuguese in Canton & Macao
Manchu occupation 1637
Tibet conquered 1750
Opium wars
Taiping Rebellion 1850-1864
Sino-Japanese War 1894-1895
Boxer Rebellion 1900
Sun Yat-sen, Rep. 1912
Manchukuo Japanese
Communist China 1948
Cultural Revolution
Border clashes with U.S.S.R.
U.S. recognizes Communist China 1979

KOREA
Mongol invasions
Korean renaissance
Li dynasty (to 20th century)
Japanese invasions
Korea opened to West 1876
Annexed by Japan 1910
Divided Korea
Korean War 1950

JAPAN / ASHIKAGA SHOGUNATE 1336-1568 / TOKUGAWA SHOGUNATE 1600-1868 / JAPANESE EMPIRE
Feudal Kamakura period 1185-1333
Mongol invasions
Civil wars
First Portuguese visit
St. Francis Xavier
Tokyo capital
Christianity introduced
Perry's visit 1854
Russo-Japanese War 1904-1905
World War I 1914
Showa Period 1926
World War II
Economic prosperity

SOUTHEAST ASIA / PACIFIC ISLANDS
Thai migrations
Maoris to N.Z.
Thai Kdm. at Ayutthaya 1350-1767
Decline of Khmers
Fall of Madjapahit Kdm. in Java
Burma united
Magellan 1521
Dutch found Batavia 1619
Rangoon founded
Thai Kdm. at Bangkok
Raffles founds Singapore 1819
French & Brit. protectorates
Australia and New Zealand dominion status
S.E. ASIAN STATES
Indep. of S.E. Asian States
Vietnam Conflict 1959-1975
New Pacific nations

Map: EMPIRE OF GENGHIS KHAN
MONGOLIA — TURKESTAN — ARABIA — PERSIA — TIBET — INDIA

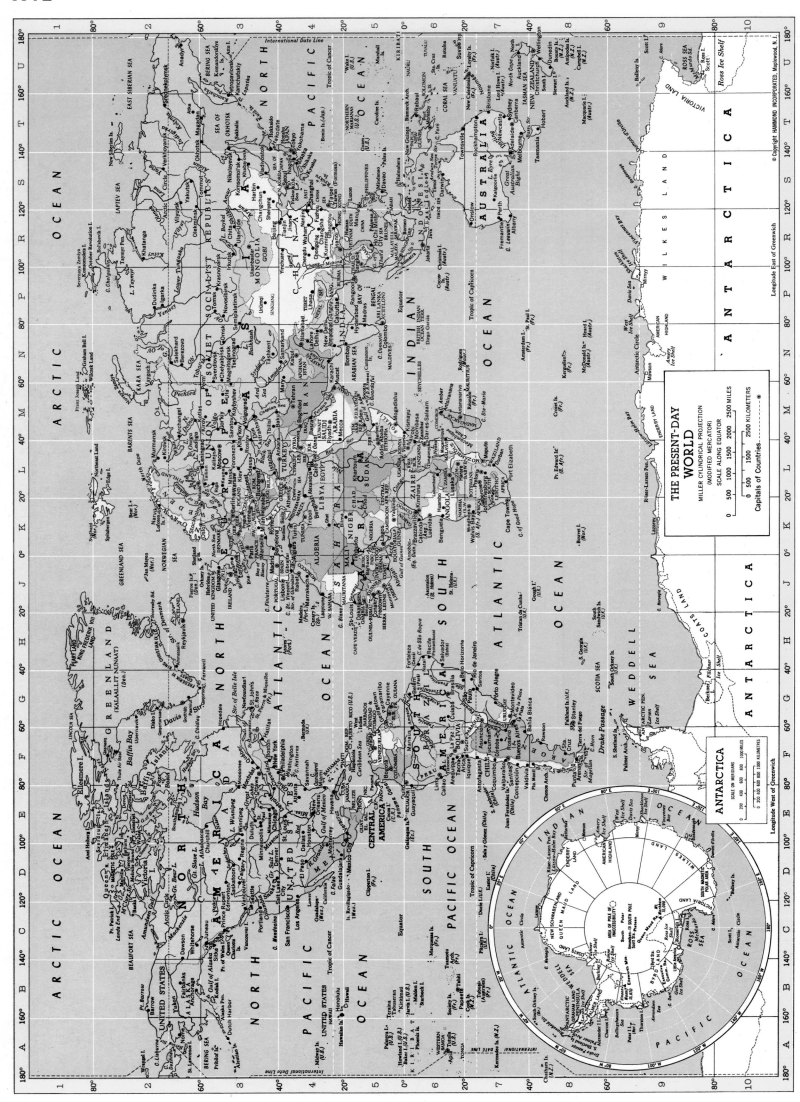

THE PRESENT-DAY WORLD

MILLER CYLINDRICAL PROJECTION
(MODIFIED MERCATOR)

SCALE ALONG EQUATOR

0 500 1000 1500 2000 2500 MILES
0 500 1000 1500 2500 KILOMETERS

Capitals of Countries............●

ANTARCTICA

SCALE ON MERIDIANS

0 200 400 600 800 1000 MILES
0 200 400 600 800 1000 KILOMETERS

© Copyright HAMMOND INCORPORATED, Maplewood, N.J.